[illegible] and quicken and purify the ideal [illegible]

[illegible] and Gandhism are based on different [illegible] world views. Therefore there is [illegible] remarks of the Marxists that the [illegible] characterized by religious and [illegible] and subjective illusion, is an [illegible] progressive social philosophy. [illegible] has, in a way, admitted at several [illegible] *of the Philosophy of Gandhi* that his [illegible] with their basic premises. Hence it [illegible] purpose to dispute the Marxist criticism [illegible] premises, since such arguments are bound [illegible] the attempt being made here is to [illegible] necessary clarifications to remove [illegible] support some modern [illegible] claim to be no less rational than [illegible] themselves to be.

STUDIES IN GANDHIAN THOUGHT AND MARXISM

WITH SPECIAL REFERENCE TO VINOBA BHAVE

Studies in Gandhian Thought and Marxism

With Special Reference to Vinoba Bhave

VISHWANATH TANDON

NATIONAL GANDHI MUSEUM
New Delhi – 110002

in association with

RADHA PUBLICATIONS
New Delhi – 110002

First edition 2006

ISBN : 81-7487-451-8

Price Rs. 650/-

Published by
The Director
National Gandhi Museum
Rajghat, New Delhi - 110002
Phones: 23311793, 23310168, 23328310
Fax: 91-011-23311793
e-mail: gandhimk@nda.vsnl.net.in
website: www.gandhimuseum.org

in association with

Radha Publications
4231/1, Ansari Road
Daryaganj, New Delhi - 110002
Phones: 23247003, 23254306
Fax: 91-011-23254306

Composed by
Sai Graphic Design
8694, D.B. Gupta Road,
Paharganj, New Delhi - 110055
Phone: 9868011398

Contents

Contents

Preface

I have been a student all my life. Brought up in the Gandhian age whom good fortune also brought in some contact with Gandhiji and Vinobaji, I was naturally attracted towards their thinking. My profession as a teacher helped me in it, and this book is the outcome of my efforts to understand them and the urge in me to share my understanding with others, for what it is worth.

Sometime in the later seventies when the Publications Division of the Government of India published the correspondence of Romain Rolland and Gandhiji and when I read in it the former writing to Soumendranath Tagore that "the role I have assumed in today's battles, which you in your youthful intransigence will no doubt find hard to understand, is to try to be a link between the two revolutions, Gandhi's and Lenin's, so that the two may come together at this hour to overthrow the old world and found a new order", a desire was roused in me to make a comparative study of both, taking Gandhiji in the broader sense by including Vinoba and Jayaprakash Narayan in it.

It was about this very period that I had come to read Madhu Dandavate's *Marx and Gandhi* (1977), Madhu Limaye's *Marxvad and Gandhivad* (1981), a compilation of Acharya Narendra Deva's *Towards a Socialist Society* (1979) and

Jayaprakash Narayan's statement: "I have learnt both from Gandhi and Lenin to work among the people. In my ideas there is a synthesis of both the revolutionaries." This led me to begin my study with Vinoba in the context of Marx and, to examine later how Narendra Deva, Dandavate and Limaye have tried to synthesize between the two, and finally to end with the study of Jayaprakash Narayan's transition from what he himself termed as "From Socialism to Sarvodaya" and to get an idea of his "Total Revolution" as a synthesis between Gandhiji and Lenin.

Thus my search began with Vinobaji and I wrote three articles on him in Hindi which were published by the Hindi *Gandhi Marg* under the titles of "Vinoba aur Marx" (September 1982), "Marxvadi aur Vinobaji" (February 1983), and "Marxvadi Alochana ki Samiksha" (March 1983), and then the fourth article on "Bharatiya Samajvad: Marx se Gandhi ki Oar" (November 1983). My Hindi writing stopped there and I started preparing chapters for an English book titled *Sarvodaya and Marxism*. The plan was to have three chapters on Vinoba and two chapters on Jayaprakash Narayan, with a connecting chapter on Romain Rolland. All the other chapters had been prepared except the last one on "Total Revolution", which I could not write though the material for that had been collected, since I was called upon to do some more urgent work. Of the prepared chapters, the one on Vinoba and Marx and that on Romain Rolland were published in the issues of July 1987 and October-December 2002 of *Gandhi Marg*.

With the passage of time and my advanced age, I gave up the former idea and wrote to the National Gandhi Museum to find out if it would be interested in publishing a book on

Vinoba and Marx containing three chapters on Vinoba along with two 1941 speeches of Vinoba relevant to the topic and three appendices on "Vinoba and the Theory of Trusteeship", a "Vinoba and Satyagraha" and "The Bhoodan–Gramdan Movement (1951-74)–A Review" which had also appeared as articles in the *Gandhi Marg*. Since it was willing to consider, I sought the permission to include the two speeches of Vinoba translated by me from their Hindi version in the proposed publication from Sri Ranjit Desai, Convenor, Gram Seva Mandal, Gopuri (Wardha), the holder of the copyright of Vinoba's speeches and writings. Sri Desai was kind enough to accord it and I am grateful to him for it.

Then it occurred to me that first chapter should deal with Gandhiji and after much thinking, I prepared it under the title of "Gandhi, Marx and Marxists", and sent the whole material to Dr. Y.P. Anand, Director of the National Gandhi Museum, for consideration. He looked into it and felt that the two chapters of "Marxists and Vinoba" and "Marxist Criticism Examined", written some two decades back, needed some revision and that since the matter also takes Gandhiji into account, some change in the title was also needed. There was force in his suggestions and hence the change in the title and revision of the two chapters of which the latter was even rewritten. A casual remark of his also led me to deal in the "Introduction" the humanist Marx of whom not many are aware.

I am very happy that Dr. Y.P. Anand found it worth publishing and I am obliged to him both for his valuable suggestions and for undertaking its publication. I may also thank those persons of the Museum Library who helped in its publication in their own way, in particular Sri S.K. Bhatnagar, the Head of the Library. I am also grateful to my old friend, Sri N. Vasudevan for his labour of love in helping in the proof-reading.

1159 Ratan Lal Nagar
Kanpur 208 022
December 25, 2005

VISHWANATH TANDON

Publisher's Note

Essential ideas and thoughts of Mahatma Gandhi, Karl Marx and Vinoba Bhave will last irrespective of the fast changes in technology and politico-economic structures all over the world. It is so because their philosophies deal with issues that are basic to the functioning of human societies. Therefore, it is necessary to delve into these from varied perspectives again and again in order to improve our understanding of the current driving instincts, social forces and conflicts, and problems and their likely solutions. Both Karl Marx and Mahatma Gandhi had not only given entirely new directions for human societies but also brought about and led vast revolutionary movements in their times. Both they and their times are past but the strength of their ideas and actions has left permanent impress on human social order and are again and again referred to as relevant to the emerging social issues.

It is in this context that this book, written by Dr. Vishwanath Tandon, a dedicated scholar on Mahatma Gandhi and Vinoba Bhave — a book which contrasts the Gandhian and Marxian thoughts, as based on the erudite perceptions of Vinoba Bhave, — is being published by the National Gandhi Museum, New Delhi.

Vinoba Bhave had written in 1950 in his 'Introduction' to K.G. Mashruwala's thesis 'Gandhi and Marx': "What can be a more fascinating study — than that of comparison between the ideologies of Gandhi, the great soul (*Mahatma*), and Marx, the great thinker (*Mahamuni*)?"

Dr. Vishwanath Tandon, now 93 years old, has written this scholarly study, titled "Studies in Gandhian Thought and Marxism With Special Reference to Vinoba Bhave", giving a historical view-point on the Marxist thought — particularly from the Gandhian perspective. It is hoped that serious students of Marxist and Gandhian thoughts will find this work of interest. This Museum remains deeply obliged to Dr. Vishwanath Tandon for his devoted efforts to compile and finalize this work in spite of his failing health.

7 February 2006 **Dr. Y.P. ANAND**

Director

National Gandhi Museum

Rajghat, New Delhi-110002

Introduction

The title of the book is likely to raise two questions in the mind of an onlooker, in particular if he or she be in his or her twenties. The first is as to who is this Vinoba? Is he such as to say something special about Marxism? This question would be quite natural for them since Vinoba died more than twenty years back and there is no memorial of his in the memorial city of Delhi to make the media keep him alive by reporting functions on his birth and death anniversaries. It is not that they are not observed but it is done at his ashram at Paunar, some seven miles off from the city of Wardha on the road to Nagpur, but those functions are hardly reported outside Vidarbha or Maharashtra.

The second question relates to Marxism itself and it may also partly relate to Gandhian thought as well. It may be asked if Marxism still got any importance when the states or countries professing it both in theory and practice are giving it up and it appears to be a dying ideology. The same may be said of Gandhian thought since leaving a small number of people, the rest of the country appears to have repudiated Gandhiji and his thought, only to remember him formally on certain days of the year. In the words of Dr. J.D. Sethi, "In his own life-time Gandhi was abused in very harsh terms not only by the imperialists but also by orthodox Hindus and Jains, by the westernized upper class educated elite, by Muslim and

Anglo-Indian leaders and not the least by the Marxists. That was perhaps a less absurd situation than that of the present one, as said earlier, Gandhi is both worshipped as a father figure and dismissed or interpreted without being read."[1]

These questions have to be answered and I take up Vinoba first. He was a person whose personality and opinion Gandhiji valued most. He wrote to his father when Vinoba joined his ashram at the age of about twenty-one: "Your son Vinoba is with me. Your son acquired at so tender an age such high spiritedness (spirituality) and asceticism as took of me years of patient labours to."[2] This speaks of his spiritual attainments, while his choice of Vinoba as the first Satyagrahi for the Individual Satayaraha of 1940 in preference to Jawaharlal Nehru, the second Satyagrahi, speaks of his nearness to Gandhiji in the field of thought and action. Gandhiji had even thought him capable of writing a treatise on the science of satyagraha[3] and after his death his constructive work followers requested Vinoba to guide them and it was endorsed by all including the topmost Gandhians present in their conference in March 1948.

Vinoba's personality was a very rare one. With an exceptionally sharp mind and excellent memory, he would go here and there through a bulky volume in fifteen or twenty minutes, get its gist and then would put it aside for ever, ready to answer any question on it. While still a high school and intermediate student in Baroda, he had read all the biographies in the State Library with titles from A to Z, hundreds of other books including the Oxford Dictionary but excluding romances, plays and poems. While once in a jail, he asked a communist fellow prisoner to read out to him his literature and its deep knowledge that he thereby acquired even surprised his near colleagues. Sri Aurobindo had presented a copy of his *The Life Divine* to Gandhiji. He passed it on to Vinoba saying that since he would not be able to spare time for reading it, he should go through it and later tell him about it. Hence it was not surprising that he was requested to write an Introduction to K.G. Mashruwala's *Gandhi and Marx* and he wrote quite a long introduction to it. And later, his Bhoodan movement brought him in touch with many communists and in his talks with them and on many other occasions, he dealt with Marxism and communist ideology from time to time. Many of his relevant utterances had been compiled and published in Hindi under the title of *Sarvodaya aur Samyavad*. Thus there is enough material on the subject, both compiled and published and uncompiled but available in his lectures (*pravachans*), in mimeographed form mostly published.

Such had been Vinoba, a great thinker and a great constructive worker between whose thought and action there was no gulf. Gandhiji had been one of the three persons who influenced him most, other two being Adi Shankaracharya and Saint Jnaneshwar. He was, however, a man of his own ideas and it has been truly said about him by Hallam Tennyson: "Like a candle lit at a neighbouring flame, he now burns with a steady and separate light."[4]

So much about Vinoba, and now about Marx and Marxism. Every thought has its temporary and permanent elements and it is the latter which keeps it alive. Marxism is not devoid of it. It was for nothing that Vinoba said of him: "If anyone since the Buddha raised the voice of the poor and the afflicted out of compassion, it is Marx."[5] Referring to his call to the poor (working days) of the world to unite for they had nothing to lose but their chains, Vinoba had said that it was an important idea given by him.[6] Gandhiji too was appreciative of his concern for the poor as we would see later in the next chapter. As George Catlin said, "He (Gandhiji) was not an anti-Marxist", though he contrasts their ideas and finds them standing poles apart.[7]

The problems of inequality and exploitation in their various forms still loom large before the world, both within the countries and between the countries and they can only be neglected at great peril. On this issue, both Gandhian thought and Marxism are one though their methods of their removal differ. But as we would see later, it is not the only thing common to both, and it would be wrong to think that Marxism now stands discredited. What has been discredited is not Marxism but the Leninist interpretation of it, which had been influenced both by Russian history and the backward economy of Russia.[8] According to Harold Laski, that interpretation was not in accord with the thinking of either Marx or Engels and its results were tragic. It led both the communists inside and outside Russia to insist that that interpretation was the only way of understanding the world.[9]

To do justice to Lenin it may, however, be mentioned that there are many thinkers who impute the unfortunate consequences of that interpretation to Stalin. Lenin was aware of the defects of his character and in his political testament had advised his removal from secretaryship.[10] Moreover, there was an elasticity in Lenin which is apparent from his New Economic Policy and his view about the national movements in subject countries as against the view of M.N. Roy, which makes one hold that had he not died so early in 1924, he would have attempted to minimise the evil consequences of his interpretation. Whatever be the correct view, what we know is that after the death of Stalin, as time passed, communism came to be divided in various schools of thought—Chinese communism, Eurocommunism and that of Yugoslavia, and by the nineties, the East European countries had started throwing it off and also asserting their independence of Moscow. It happened because communism failed to fulfil the rising expectations of the peoples there, while capitalism in the West was successful in it.[11] It also affected Soviet Union, all the more so since its defence budget, to keep pace with the USA, was telling upon its economy. This explains the rise of Michail Gorbachev there. According to Mohit Sen, though the Soviet Russia had achieved a historic success in industrialization to make backward Russia into a model power in an incredibly short time, its costs were too high in human and material terms. It had also led to the growth of bureaucracy and bureaucratic mindset with their concomitant evils like corruption, growth of hierarchy and vested interests.[12] Concerning Gorbachev, Madhu Limaye says: "There was a time when communists imbued with the Stalinist spirit, talked of class morality, of relativist ethics, and of end justifying the means, and totally ignored the context of upward moving human spirit and the growing store of universal human values. Gorbachev not only highlights the dangers of a nuclear holocaust, he has also sought to restore the broad humanistic perspective and framework for a struggle for a new social order".[13] Regarding the overall consequences of it, he had said elsewhere that "the Soviet communists do not anymore speak of war as an opportunity for revolution. They do not talk of violent revolution. They accept a peaceful transition and the building up of a democratic state. They want a nonviolent order. They now recognize that crude and violent means can corrupt any goal".[14]

All this, however, had been a matter of slow realization for the communist world, but there had been thinkers who had been emphasizing the humanism of Marx's ideas of which only some may be aware of since the Leninist interpretation of Marx still dominates the general mind. They do it on the basis of Marx's *Economic and Philosophical Manuscripts* of 1844 which had not been published till 1932. An eminent German philosopher, Ernst Bloch (1885-1977) relied upon it and his exposition of the human aspect of Marxism had earned for him the resentment of the Russian Marxists. He was of the view that Marxian philosophy is "a philosophy of the future" and Marx was an utopian. Bloch sought "to infuse the socialist psychology with the humanism of early Marx" and worked "to infuse the contemporary Marxism with the most emancipatory and the utopian element of young Marx."[15]

Another prominent thinker to project Marx as a humanist was the Hungarian philosopher Georg Lukacs (1885-1971). He refuted all forms of determinism and reductionism and held that Marx's dialectical materialism was not a dogmatic study of external laws but a method of enquiry.[16] There were some others too who laid stress on the humanism of Marx, but of all of them Erich Fromm (1900-1980) is probably the most prominent. A German psychologist, who migrated to USA in 1934, he was a prolific writer whose many books refer to Marx and his humanist thinking. He himself belongs to the category of humanist socialists whose socialism while based on Marx differs from both the Soviet and Chinese communism. He is of particular interest to us since many of his ideas remind us of Gandhian thinking though they appear to be independent of Gandhiji whose name probably occurs nowhere in any of his books, though he mentions E.F. Schumacher with approval. He deserves being dealt here at some length.

Erich Fromm wrote in 1967: "One of the most remarkable phenomenon of the past decade has been the renaissance of humanism in the various ideological systems."[17] Humanism, according to him, believes in the unity of the human race and in man's capacity to perfect himself by his own efforts. Over the ages, some humanists have believed in the goodness of man or in the existence of God, while others have not. But all of them have believed in the possibility of man's perfectibility and because of their belief in the unity of mankind, they never became fanatics.[18]

He counts Marx among humanists and says that he was the first to declare that theory cannot be separated from practice, knowledge from action and the spiritual aims from the social systems. Marx held that a free and independent man could exist only in an economic and social system that, by its rationality and abundance, brought to an end the epoch of pre-history and the epoch of human history which would make the full development of the individual the condition for the full development of society. According to him, Marxism was perhaps the strongest spiritual movement of a broad non-theistic nature in the nineteenth century Europe, but after 1914—or even before—most of this spirit disappeared.[19] He even says: "Western social democrats and their bitter opponents, communists within and without the Soviet Union, transformed socialism into a purely economic concept, the goal of which was maximum consumption, maximum use of machines."[20] As against it, socialism for Marx meant a society which serves the 'true' needs of men and he differentiated between the true needs and artificially created needs. True needs are those whose fulfillment is necessary for the realisation of one's true essence as a human being. And his idea of full self-realization was that it could only occur in his relatedness to the world and to fellow men and the relationship of men to women.[21] In this context, Fromm also says: "The productive, free, independent, loving individual—that was his (Marx's) vision of man. He was not concerned with maximum production and consumption, although he was in favour of making possible for everybody the attainment of an economic level that is the basis of a humanly dignified life. He was also not primarily concerned with the equalization of income, although he would have been opposed to such inequality as prevents men from sharing the same basic experiences of life. Marx's central concern was the liberation of man from the kind of work which destroys his individuality, transforms him into a thing, and enslaves him to the things of his own creation."[22]

The problem of alienation is often referred to by sociologists. Dr J.D. Sethi says: "Alienation is the most serious and pervasive problem of modern human societies, more particularly of the developed societies, both capitalist and communist."[23] He finds Marx talking of three kinds of alienation, namely alienation of the worker from his product, his self-alienation and the alienation of men from each other in social relations. Gandhiji added to it three other alienations, completing the picture. They are alienation of man from nature, alienation from his inner self and alienation of consumption from production.[24] Fromm, however, says: "For Marx, alienation in the process of work, from the product of work and from circumstances, is inseparably connected with alienation from oneself, from one's fellow man and from nature."[25]

Fromm explains Marx's opposition to religion as due to its being alienated. He says that Marx's fight was against the idol of God. He had expressed his concern for man's soul, though not theistically but in philosophical language. His atheism is the most advanced form of rational mysticism closer to Meister Eckhart and Zen Buddhism.[26] Similarly, he has an explanation for Marx's reference to force and revolution which appear to sanction what happened in Russia. Fromm says that the idea of political revolution was not specifically Marx's idea. It has been the idea of bourgeois society during the last three hundred years. Because this class believed that the seizure of political power by the people was the solution of the social problem, political revolution was seen as a means to the attainment of freedom. Marx's mistake was that he did not free himself from the traditional overvaluation of political power and force. However, he made an improvement over that tradition. He saw that political force cannot produce anything for which there is no preparation in the political and social process. Force can only give the last push to a development which has virtually already taken place. "Force", he said, "is the midwife of every old society pregnant with a new one."[27]

Fromm, however, has pointed to several mistakes made by Marx. At one place, he refers to three of them which were the result of his under-estimation of the complexity of human nature. The first was the neglect of moral factor in man because of his assumption that the goodness of man would assert itself automatically when the economic changes have been achieved. He did not think that a better society could not be brought into life by people who had not themselves undergone a moral change. Secondly, he misjudged the situation and became hopeful of the realization of socialism.[28] In this context, Fromm says: "Both he and Engels thought that capitalism has already reached the end of its possibilities and hence, the revolution was just around the corner. But they were thoroughly mistaken, as Engels had to state after Marx's death."[29] Thirdly, his conception that socialization of the means of production was not only necessary but also sufficient condition for the transformation of the capitalist society into a socialist cooperative society, was wrong.[30]

To any criticism of his reliance on the *Economic and Philosophical Manuscripts* of 1844 in preference to the later works of Marx, Fromm's reply was: "It is true that Marx (like Engels) in the course of his lifetime changed some of his ideas and concepts. He became more adverse to the use of terms too close to Hegelian idealism; his language became less enthusiastic and eschatological; probably he was also more discouraged in the later years of his life than he was in 1844. But in spite of certain changes in his concepts, in mood, in language, the core of the philosophy developed by young Marx was never changed, and it is impossible to understand his concept of socialism, and his criticism of capitalism as developed in his later years, except on the basis of his concept of man which he developed in his earlier writings."[31]

It would be well to close this discussion of humanist Marx in the words of Fromm himself. He writes: "If Marx had pronounced his ideas today, at the beginning—and rapidly increasing—decline of capitalism, his *real* message would have a chance to be influential or even victorious, provided one can make such a historical conjecture. As it is, even the word 'socialism' and 'communism' are compromised. At any rate, every socialist or communist party that could claim to represent Marxian thought would have to be based on the conviction that the Soviet regimes are not socialist system in any sense, that socialism is incompatible with a bureaucratic thing-centred consumption oriented social system, that it is incompatible with the materialism and cerebralization that characterize the Soviet, like the capitalist, system."[32]

So, it would be wrong to confine Marx to his Leninist interpretation and to consider him to be outdated. There is enough of permanent and abiding in his thought to make it relevant to a lesser or greater degree.

NOTES AND REFERENCES

1. J.D. Sethi, *Gandhian Values and 20th Century Challenges* (Publications Division, Govt. of India, New Delhi, 1979), p. 2.
2. Cited in Suresh Ram, *Vinoba and His Mission* (Sarva Seva Sangh Prakashan, Kashi, 1961), p. 15.
3. *Harijan*, March 3, 1946.
4. Cited in P.D. Tandon (ed.), *Vinoba Bhave: The Man and His Mission* (Vora & Co., Bombay, 1952), p. 98.
5. *Vinoba Pravachan*, September 25, 1957.
6. *Vinoba Pravachan*, July 11, 1957.
7. S. Radhakrishnan (ed.), *Mahatma Gandhi* (Jaico Publishing House, Bombay, 1956), p. 286.
8. F.W. Coker, *Recent Political Thought* (D. Appleton Century Company, New York, 1934), refers to the influence of history on p. 140 while the influence of backward economy has been referred to by many.
9. Introduction to *Communist Manifesto: Socialist Landmark* (Allen and Unwin, London, 1954,), p. 82.
10. Sidney Hook, *Marx and Marxists* (Euresia Publishing House, New Delhi, 1966), p. 108.
11. K.M. Pannikar's article in *Patriot*, November 4, 1989.
12. Mohit Sen, *Assessing Stalin and Stalinism*, in *Mainstream*, Annual, 1988.
13. Madhu Limaye, *Significance of Changes in Soviet Union*, in ibid.
14. *Mainstream*, December 16, 1989.
15. Article on him in Elizabeth Devine and three others (Eds.), *Thinkers of the 20th Century* (Himalayan Books, New Delhi, 1987).
16. Article on him in ibid.
17. Introduction in Erich Fromm (ed.), *Socialist Humanism: An*

International Symposium (Allen Lane, The Penguin Press, London, 1967).
18. ibid.
19. ibid.
20. Erich Fromm, *To Have Or To Be* (Bantam Books, New York, 1982), p. 143.
21. Erich Fromm (ed.), *Marx's Concept of Man* (Frederick Ungar Publishing House, New York, 1972), p. 62 and his *Man May Prevail* (Allen and Unwin, London, 1962), p. 72.
22. *Man May Prevail*, pp. 72-73.
23. J.D. Sethi, op. cit., p. 35.
24. ibid., pp. 35-36.
25. *Marx's Concept of Man*, p. 58.
26. ibid., pp. 63-64.
27. ibid., p. 24 and his *The Sane Society* (Routledge, London, 1956), p. 261.
28. *The Sane Society*, p. 264.
29. *To Have Or To Be*, p. 143.
30. *The Sane Society*, p. 265.
31. *Marx's Concept of Man*, p. 79.

    It would be appropriate to point out here what a CPI scholar, Hiren Mukerjee, has to say about it. He remarks: "It is only to be expected that in the writings of the young Marx, represented somewhat strikingly in his recently unearthed *Economic and Philosophical Manuscripts* of 1844, the accent was on man. Herein Marx declared that if 'communism' is the riddle of history solved, it was because 'communism, as fully developed naturalism, equals humanism.' These Manuscripts have given rise to a storm of debate, in which not only Marxist thinkers have taken part but others also, who have tried to project the idea of a conflict between the thought of the young and the old Marx, the former allegedly being concerned with the 'human essence' and the latter unworried about the problems of man and his freedom. There is no room here for a discussion of this issue, but it seems to be plain that Marx's ideas on this and other related subjects were an organic whole. Even in *Capital*, Marx did not hesitate to posit 'alienation', as he understood it, as a key element in his system." (*Remembering Marx*, a CPI Publication, 1967, pp. 81-82).
32. *To Have Or To Be*, pp. 144-45.

PART ONE

Vinoba and Marx

CHAPTER ONE

Gandhi, Marx and Marxists

The last two decades of the 19th century when Gandhiji was a student in Great Britain were a period when that country was astir with a new life. It witnessed, in particular, the rise of socialist ideas. The first volume of Marx's *Das Kapital* had appeared in its English translation in 1887. The Independent Labour Party was born the same year and the Fabian Society, established in 1884 was popularizing socialist ideas. But Gandhiji appears to be oblivious of them. He showed interest in persons and societies connected with activities having some relationship with Indian culture. His indifference towards socialist ideas has been attributed by B.R. Nanda, with some justification, to his energies being devoted to the observance of the three pledges he had given to his mother concerning abstinence from meat, wine and woman during his stay there.[1] But it seems that a greater reason for it must have been their irrelevance to the then India, a subject and unindustrialized country, to which he was to return for his legal practice. This is corroborated, in a way, by Nanda himself in another book of his where he mentions that the political leaders of India had not taken any cognizance of socialist ideas before the Russian Revolution of 1917.[2]

However, while he was in South Africa, his attention had been drawn to the events in Russia of 1905. There were probably three reasons for it. First, he had read Tolstoy's *The Kingdom of God Is Within You* and it must have aroused his interest both in Tolstoy and in his country. Secondly, many of his white associates there must have been keenly interested in Russian events and he came to share their interest in them. Lastly, there was something in Maxim Gorky and the Russian Revolution of 1905 which were of special interest to him, as we learn from the four articles about them which he wrote in the *Indian Opinion* in 1905. Gorky had greatly impressed Gandhiji since in spite of having been brought up in extreme poverty he had become an eminent writer, feared by the Czar's government and imprisoned by it — which Gorky took as an honour. As regards the 1905 Revolution which had compelled the Czar's government to concede that no law would be enacted without the people's consent, Gandhiji had been impressed by the method of the strike resorted to in it with success. He was of the view that even if the government there failed to keep its words and the people were unable to compel it to do so, it would not show that their method was wrong while, in case of success, the Revolution would be regarded as the greatest political event of the century.[3]

Gandhiji finally returned to India in 1915 and a year later he became actively involved in the problems facing this country which led him to the Non-Cooperation Movement of 1921. All this left him with no energy and time to take any interest in the Russian Revolution of 1917 though he must have been aware of it. However, as far as the country was concerned, the immediate effect of that Revolution was the birth of a few labour unions in 1918 and 1919, the formation of the All India Trade Union Congress and a book, *Gandhi and Lenin* by S.A. Dange.[4] The popularity of the 1921 Movement did not permit any further progress of the communist ideas in the country till its withdrawal and failure which greatly disappointed the people. The Communist Party of India itself came into existence in 1924 outside India as an organ of the World Communist Movement.[5] All this led to the growth of the leftist ideas in the Congress under the leadership of Jawaharlal Nehru and Subhas Chandra Bose.

Gandhiji, however, did not take any interest in communist ideas. He read a lot of books during his imprisonment in 1922-24 but they included no Marxian literature. The first communist to meet him was S.D. Saklatwala, a communist member of British Parliament, in 1927. The talks with him had centred round multiplicity of wants and the modern rush for it. Gandhiji had then said to him: "I am sorry but we do stand at opposite poles. There is, however, one great thing in common between us. Both claim to have the good of the country and humanity as our only goal. Though we may for the moment seem to be going in opposite directions. I expect we shall meet one day."[6]

Gandhiji's first comments on Soviet Russia were made in 1928. Speaking at the Gujarat Vidyapeeth, he had said: "I must confess that I have not been able to understand Bolshevism. All I know is that it aims at the abolition of the institution of private property. This is an application of the ethical ideal of non-possession in the realm of economics, and if the people adopted this ideal of their own accord or could be made to accept it by means of peaceful persuasion, there could be nothing like it. But from what I know of Bolshevism, it not only does not preclude the use of force but freely sanctions it for the appropriation of private property and for maintaining the collective ownership of the same. And if it is so, I have no hesitation in saying that the Bolshevik regime in its present form cannot last for long. For it is my firm conviction that nothing enduring can be built on violence. But be that as it may, there is no questioning of the fact that the Bolshevik ideal has behind it the purest sacrifice of countless men and women who have given up their all for its sake, and an idea sanctified by the sacrifices of such master spirit as Lenin cannot go in vain, the noble example of their renunciation will be emblazoned for ever and quicken and purify the ideal as time passes."[7]

Lenin's attitude towards the national movements in subject countries was not un-favourable. But after his death in 1924 the opposite view according priority to anti-capitalism over anti-imperialism came to prevail, and the Communist Party of India (CPI) under the control of the International Communist Movement (Comintern), did the same. Hence its view of Gandhiji was totally against him. The 1929 edition of Soviet Encyclopedia had described Gandhiji as "a great reactionary who hails from the Bania caste; betrayed the people and helped the imperialists against them,"[8] and so on. The Indian Communists also felt the same and such a view of Gandhiji persisted till his end. However, after the rise of Hitler and Stalin's realization of its danger, the communist policy became of infiltration into the Congress which they succeeded in doing through the Congress Socialist Party (CSP) formed in 1934. They were, however, expelled from the CSP in 1940 when they came to adopt a pro-war attitude.[9]

Gandhiji must have been aware of the view held by the communists about him, but he never allowed it to create any bitterness in him about them. Philip Spratt, who had been a communist at one time, writes: "Gandhi often discussed his views with the communists. As with all opponents, he wished to sustain good relations with them. He was appreciative and professed to accept their ultimate aim of equality, though he never abandoned his objection to violence and untruth, which imply a breach of good relations."[10]

Though outwardly it appeared that his differences with them lay on the question of means since Gandhiji held that ends do not justify means and that wrong means can never lead to good results, with his consequent emphasis on nonviolence in its positive sense, his differences with the communists were fundamental, going beyond the question of means. Jayantanuja Bandyopadhyaya says that Gandhiji "geared all his ideological thinking to the same ultimate values (as those of Marx and Engels) although his values have deeper metaphysical moorings than those of Marxism."[11] And it may also be mentioned here that though Gandhiji could only find time to read Marx, Lenin and Stalin during his last incarceration in the Aga Khan Palace in Pune (1942-44), he had been expressing his thinking, in one context or the other, on their ideas from time to time.

Gandhiji's experiences had led him to believe that a fuller life was impossible without a belief in a Divine Law. He had felt that a person lacking that faith is like drop of ocean bound to perish.[12] A firm believer in God, he once said: "God is that undefinable something which we all feel but which we do not know. To me God is Truth and Love. God is Ethics and Morality. God is fearlessness. God is the source of light and life and yet He is above and beyond all these. He is conscience. He is even the atheism of the atheist."[13] To the question if He is benevolent or malevolent, his answer was: "I see it as purely benevolent, for I see that in the midst of death life persists, in the midst of untruth truth persists, in the midst of darkness light persists."[14] Because of such a conception of his about God, he even regarded such self-proclaimed atheists as Charles Bradlaugh and Ramachandra Rao Gora as theists. He once said to the latter, "You may call yourself as atheist, but as long as you feel akin with mankind, you accept God in practice."[15]

Marx looked upon religion as an opiate and it does not lack justification altogether, besides its other defect of being commonly identified with narrow-minded creeds and dogmas. But Gandhiji, in spite of its prevailing defects, still stood for it, identifying it with morality, which meant to him "the desire to improve ourselves for the sake of doing good to others." The higher moral law for him was to "unremittingly work for the good of mankind." He also rejected all religious doctrines which did not appeal to reason.[16] Hence as B.R. Nanda says: "Gandhi had a strongly rational and sceptical streak which enabled him to fashion for himself a religious philosophy, which though grounded in Hinduism, acquired a deeply humanist and cosmopolitan complexion."[17]

While Gandhiji did not deny the value of economics in the life and thought of individuals and groups, he stood for economic equality, though he did not support the method of class struggle for the abolition of classes and for establishing economic equality. In a reply to a correspondent, he had said that he was "wrong in suggesting that I do not believe in the existence of class struggle. What I do not believe in is the necessity of fomenting and keeping it alive."[18] He believed that it was perfectly possible to avoid it, and those who talked of class war as inevitable, did not either understand the implication of nonviolence or their understanding of it was skin-deep.[19] Among the nonviolent methods advocated by him for the purpose, one was his principle of trusteeship which was a broader concept embracing all that a person has including his wealth, energy, time and talents. They were all to be devoted to the service of others, in particular those who were not fortunately placed. As such, it aimed in its economic aspects at the abolition of economic inequality and the establishment of a classless society, something which the Marxists desired to achieve by violent expropriations of the wealthy. Clarifying the idea behind it, Gandhiji had once said: "They (capitalists) know that I desire to end capitalism almost, if not quite as much as the most advanced socialists or even communists. But our methods differ. My theory of 'trusteeship' is no make-shift, certainly no camouflage. I am confident that it will survive all theories. It has the sanction of philosophy and religion behind it."[20] Hence the communists were wrong when they interpreted it as aiming to keep capitalism alive.

There is, however, something in common between Marx's view of the state and that of Gandhiji, though there are differences too. Marx's view of the state was based on his theory of class struggle. To him the state was only an instrument of domination by the economically dominant class, an instrument of exploitation in its hands. Hence he considered its abolition as a matter of prime necessity and held that it would be achieved in two stages, a prior stage of socialism and a later one of communism. The first would be characterized by the dictatorship of the proletariat in which the working class would have seized the machinery of the state and would use it to abolish private ownership of the means of production. Though Marx is silent on many points in the matter, it is for the valid reason that it is impossible to foresee many things in advance. But it is certain that he did not believe in the method of political democracy. The second stage of communism, as envisaged, was to be of a classless society which would also be stateless since with the disappearance of classes, the state was bound to disappear.[21]

Marx's conception of the two stages has been differently interpreted by the various Marxist schools of thought but what we are especially concerned with is its interpretation by the Russian Marxists. According to them, the first stage of dictatorship would be of the highest intensification of state. Lenin was of the view that the substitution of a proletarian for the capitalist state is impossible without violent revolution, and that the Paris Commune failed because it was too moderate and lenient in its immediate program of constructive action.[22]

Gandhiji too had a distrust of the state. He once said: "I look upon the increase in the power of state with the greatest fear, because, although while apparently doing good by minimizing exploitation, it does the greatest harm to mankind by destroying individuality which lies at the root of all progress." And then he also added: "The State represents violence in a concentrated and organized form. The individual has a soul, but as the State is a soulless machine, it can never be weaned from violence to which it owes its very existence."[23] His political ideal was that of an enlightened anarchy. Defining it, he had said: "In such a state everyone is his own ruler. He rules himself in such a manner that he is never a hindrance to his neighbour. In the ideal state, therefore, there is no political power because there is no State. But the ideal is never fully realized. Hence the classical statement of Thoreau that that government is best which governs the least."[24] All this had led him to support political decentralization, not as a final condition but as a programme of action. Hence his famous statement that "In this structure composed of innumerable villages, life would not be a pyramid with apex sustained by the bottom but an oceanic circle and the outermost circumference would not hold power to crush the inner circle but would give strength to all within and drive its own strength from it."[25]

Another partial resemblance between them is related to their concepts of revolution. Both went beyond the idea of political revolution. Being children of the nineteenth century, both had accepted the theory of human progress and the idea of social revolution. Enough, in this respect, has already been indicated about Marx. As regards Gandhiji, he too was nothing else but a revolutionary, keen to bring about changes in every aspect of Indian society but without uprooting it from its past since he never claimed originality for his ideas. In this, he had followed the old tradition set by other eminent Indian social and religious reformers. Acharya J.B. Kripalani says about them "The Indian genius has been pre-eminently constructive. It does not reject. It builds without destroying."[26]

All items of Gandhiji's Constructive Programme primarily aimed at building a new society. To cite Acharya Kripalani again. "As a matter of fact, the constructive programme was meant to revolutionise the nation's outlook in all the spheres of social life, social in its most comprehensive sense. Gandhiji tried to clean our life from our latrines to our souls. His was a comprehensive revolution as it was based on the revaluation of our basic values."[27] This also finds endorsement in Dr Gopi Nath Dhawan. According to him, Gandhiji "aimed at a deeper revolution, a comprehensive change in values and symbols that control human activities and institutions."[28] The revolution Gandhiji aimed at, no doubt, was a nonviolent one since "it was not a programme of seizure of power but of transformation of relationship, ending in a peaceful transfer of power."[29] Both in Marx and in Gandhi, evolution and revolution play roles in social transformations. In Marx, however, though capitalism (by its evolution) inevitably prepares the way for revolution, it does not inevitably lead to it. To achieve it, deliberate, informed and intelligent action is needed,[30] Gandhiji somewhat differed. He said: "The nations have progressed both by evolution and revolution. The one is as necessary as the other. Death, which is an eternal verity, is revolution as birth and after is slow and steady evolution." He thus appears to imply that revolution is a natural culmination of evolution. He had also then said that "progress is made by growth and gradual development and not by revolution and destruction."[31]

The whole thinking of Marx is based on his materialistic interpretation of history, which regards the economic factor as the most determining one in society. As against it, Gandhiji had put forward his nonviolent interpretation of history, also termed by one as 'spiritual interpretation.' It has been named as former since Gandhiji held that with the passage of time, human society has become gentler and more humane. He finds support for it in history, in man's advancement from the stage of cannibalism to that of chase and then to that of agriculture, in the expansion of his loyalty from oneself to the family, community and nation. All these were to him signs of diminishing *himsa* and progressing *ahimsa*. And then, all prophets and *avatars* have been teaching *ahimsa* more or less. From it all, he had come to the conclusion that man has still further to progress towards it.[32]

It has been named spiritual interpretation of history on the basis that Gandhiji had once said: "I believe that the sum total of the energy of mankind is not to bring us down but to lift us up and that is the result of the unconscious working of the law of love" and that "Human history is a ceaseless growth, an unfoldment in terms of spirituality."[33]

There had been a good deal of discussion between Gandhiji and Pyarelal on the issue of Marx's interpretation of history in the Aga Khan Palace Prison (1942-44). He had then said to Pyarelal, "I do not believe that it is *Prakriti* (the Nature) which originates and governs the thought processes of *Purusha* (the Soul)." He also did not believe that economic factors were the source of all the evils in the world or that all wars could be traced to economic causes, and he cited the example of Trojan and Rajput wars in support of his contention. He also pointed out that unexpected events also play crucial roles in history. He said: "Supposing Hitler were to die today, it would alter the whole process of current history." And then he had full faith in the beneficent power of God. In a 1934 letter to Carl Heath, he had said: "But in spite of the blackness of the horizon, I have no sense of despair in me. I believe in the existence of a beneficent power that overrides and upsets all human plans. It ever produces order out of chaos and redresses wrongs in spite of the tyranny of the tyrants."[34]

However, these differences did not mean that he had no admiration for Marx and Lenin. A 1928 statement of his on Bolshevism has already been cited which indicates his appreciation of Lenin. As regards Marx, he had found him to have risen over any narrow class consciousness. He had even said to Pyarelal: "We may critcize Marx but that he was a great man who can deny? His analysis of the social ills or the cure he prescribed for them may or may not be correct. I do not accept his theories but that much I know that the poor are being ground down. Something has got to be done for it. Marx set about to do it in his own way. He had acumen, scholarship and genius."[35] And for him, the quintessence of the teachings of Marx lay in "From each according to his capacity, to each according to his need" and "All for each and each for all."[36]

There are indications that Gandhiji had some soft corner for the Russians for courageously facing Hitler's invasion, but it had not softened him towards either their ideology or the attitude of the CPI. He told a group of Communists in 1947: "You waste your time and your energy in hair-splitting, fault-finding and picking holes. If you discover a trifling flaw anywhere, real or fancied, you exploit it to make propaganda and to spread disaffection against the government in power without even caring to make a proper inquiry. It seems to have become your stock-in-trade. . . . What to me is even more pathetic is that you regard Russia as your spiritual home. Despising Indian culture, you dream of planting the Russian system here. Food, however rich, that another person eats, cannot sustain me. I can only be sustained by what I eat. In the same way, what an outside power does gives me no satisfaction as it seems to give you."[37] He also then criticized them for talking of satyagraha without following the primary conditions attached to it, the basis of it being truth without any room for the ambiguous middle. [38]

The Indian communists, on their part, continued to hold the same view of him which they held earlier. However, it was Rajni Palme Dutt who first showed some alteration of stand. After Gandhiji's martyrdom, he wrote in March 1948 that Gandhiji's detractors "can with ease pick out his weaknesses and inconsistencies in a manner which only reveals their own pettiness and inability to understand the greatness that was in him."[39] He even appeared to be advising the communists to use Gandhiji in building their own mass movement.[40] This view of his, however, did not have any perceptible effect on the Indian communists who needed a signal from the Soviet Union, but it was not forthcoming. On the other hand, A.M. Dyakov, a leading Russian Indologist wrote: "The struggle against Gandhism — the ideology of the counter-revolutionary bourgeoisie of India—is impossible without a struggle against the authority of Gandhi, against the Gandhi's cult, without the exposure of all the activities of Gandhi who had consistently betrayed the popular movement and by this rendered tremendous service to the British existence in India."[41]

However, with the passing away of Stalin and the advent of Khrushchev, a new breeze had started blowing there. The need of India's friendship under the favourable leadership of Jawaharlal Nehru provided the needed motive and it affected the Indian communists as well. The process of rethinking began with a series of articles by E.M.S. Namboodiripad in 1954 and later by his book *The Mahatma and the Isms*, published in 1958. It examines the whole career of Gandhiji starting from his days in England to his end. It finds him to be a bourgeoisie leader but with a difference. Belonging to no particular class among them, he represented them as a whole as against any individual or group among it. He writes: "He (Gandhiji) therefore, was able to look at every problem from the point of view of the long-range interests of his class as a whole, rather than from the narrow, petty, personal or group interests of sections of the bourgeoisie."[42] Herein he also sees the greatness of Gandhiji as a typical ideological political leader of the bourgeoisie.[43]

Namboodiripad has also analysed Gandhism and one may say that his final conclusion is the same that he was not always at one with the bourgeoisie. At times, his was a minority voice.[44] All this shows the difficulty of the Indian communists to rise over their ideological orthodoxy to understand him.

As regards the Soviet Union, Bulganin and Khrushchev visited India in 1955 and then Bulganin pronounced Gandhiji as an outstanding leader who had done much for the counry.[45] And in 1956 an authoritative pronouncement in the *Soviet Asian Studies* said: "Basically, Gandhi played a positive role in the development of the national liberation movement. It was precisely as a result of Gandhi's activity as a leader of the National Congress that that organization transformed itself into a mass party. *Our conditionally negative attitude towards Gandhi's nonviolent tactics has been rejected by facts*."[46]

With time, there had been some further rethinking on the attitude towards Gandhiji. Since 1960s witnessed a split in the CPI due to differences between Soviet Union and China, those who favoured Mao's thinking, came to be designated as CPI (Marxist) while pro-Russian group continued the old designation of the CPI. The CPI brought out a book, *The Mahatma: Marxist Evaluation*, in 1977 which gives the articles of important CPI thinkers on the various aspects of Gandhiji. It is difficult to do justice to that publication in this short piece and one can only draw attention to some ideas of theirs. One may, however, say that though Gandhiji was also an enigma to them, they have tried to evaluate both his leadership and ideas respectfully, keeping in their minds their commitment to Lenin's interpretation of Marxism. S.A. Dange who writes on "Mahatma Gandhi and History" says of him that here was a great life, a great hero of history who led the masses, organized them, disciplined them and put them to battle against the alien rulers. But let the historians test their theories in regard to the phenomenon of the Mahatma and the masses, though his own answer was that Gandhiji learned from the masses and led them.[47]

Hiren Mukerjee, whose article is titled "A Unique Leader", says that Gandhiji was no mere thinker who dreamt dreams. He was a maker of men and events as well, a stupendous individual, of the Indian earth, and with extraordinary resources of strength and character. But he is critical of the simplicity of life for which Gandhiji stood, and so also of his preoccupation with his principle of 'ends and means'.[48]

S.G. Sardesai who writes on "Gandhi and the CPI", says that while even as an individual his personality was extremely complex, the broader failure of the CPI lay in not being able to grasp the role of the Indian national bourgeoisie itself in the freedom movement.[49] He is critical of the political line of the colonial thesis of the Sixth Comintern of 1928 and calls it 'clearly sectarian'. According to him, it was a period when there was a greater desire for communist cooperation on the part of Gandhiji and it was a tragedy in 1930 that "we counterpoised ourselves against Gandhi and the Indian National Congress."[50] He almost concludes his article by saying: "Such was Gandhi. Not only a man once born in an epoch, not only a man of granite courage and convictions, but because of his passionate sense of identity with the lowly and the oppressed."[51] He, however, admits that it was not possible to say what he would have done if he had lived, but he is sure that he would have always continued to stand by the poor in his own way.[52]

Mohit Sen who wrote under "Gandhism after Freedom" has something to say of Gandhiji as well and while he finds Gandhiji admiring the personality of Lenin, it is not so with Leninism. He attributes it to his prejudices and thinks that because of it India was handed over to the capitalist class.[53]

Now as regards the CPI (M), it may be pointed out that Namboodiripad belonged to this group after the split, and hence his views dealt with earlier be taken as that of the CPI (M). However, P. Sundarayya, who was the General Secretary of the CPI (M) in 1972, had made certain observations in his book *Telingana People's Struggle and Its Lessons* published that very year which deserves mention. He contradicts in it the idea of Namboodiripad justifying the role of the CPI in the Second World War. According to Sundarayya though the war had become a people's war, "our party should have actively participated in the struggle against the British refusal to form a National Government by real transfer of power and against resorting to repression. While at the same time we could have continued our campaign of educating our fighting people not to be dragged into support of Hitler's and Japanese war but preparing them to resist them."[54] He is also critical of the CPI's support to the demand of Pakistan, a topic the communists have been fighting shy of discussing. Sundarayya writes: "It was this wrong and one-sided emphasis of our Party on the need to strengthen the anti-fascist war efforts, and also the Party's wrong emphasis on the right of self-determination without simultaneously fighting the separatist slogan of Pakistan, that alienated our Party from many anti-imperialist sections and youths in our country."[55]

Sundarayya's was an official publication of the CPI (M) and it seems strange that EMS Namboodiripad who succeeded him as the Secretary General repudiated his views in his 1986 publication titled *A History of Indian Freedom Struggle* without the Party doing so formally. However, it is interesting to note that Namoodiripad's view pertaining to the war had the support of C. Rajeshwar Rao, General Secretary of the CPI while Dange's view was similar to that of Sundarayya.[56]

Now reverting back to the Soviet Union, one may say that as time passed, both the external and domestic situation compelled it to repudiate Stalinism altogether and adopt a more flexible attitude. The result of it as far as Gandhiji was concerned, was a further revised view expressed in the *Fighters of National Liberation*, published in 1983. Its first chapter deals with Gandhiji. It is highly appreciative of the role of Gandhiji in the Indian freedom struggle and gives him full credit for its anti-imperialist policy and tactics and for drawing the masses into social and political movements.[57] It is, however, skeptical of Gandhiji's deep distrust of independent revolutionary activity of the masses and his formula for guardianship (trusteeship) which Gandhiji had advocated along with that of satyagraha.[58]

There was, however, a further development in 1986 which may also be mentioned here to do full justice to the Soviet Union's perception of Gandhiji. Advent into power of Mikhail Gorbachev was rather an important event in the history of the Soviet Union. Dr J.D. Sethi, an eminent scholar of both Marxism and Gandhism, wrote in 1988: "As a Gandhian I have no illusion about the Soviet Union. The global order dominated by giant nation-states, no matter what their social systems, cannot guarantee peace. .... Yet I find something quite extraordinary in what General Secretary Mikhail Gorbachev of the Soviet Union is saying or doing. I detect serious Gandhian elements or concepts in its general approach. I do not think Gorbachev has studied Gandhi but, if he does so, he can enormously profit from the study."[59]

Sethi also mentions that when "Gorbachev signed the Delhi Declaration in 1986, the word *nonviolence* was specifically used in that declaration and since then has been constantly emphasized. It came as a surprise to most people, and many saw it as part of a new Soviet propaganda. It is not that Gorbachev had become a follower of Mahatma, but if one believes as Mahatma did, that anyone in search of truth would also become a votary of nonviolence, this belief is sheer common sense and logical."[60]

In this context, it would be interesting to see what a Soviet scholar has to say about Gandhiji in the era of Gorbachev. Dr. Martyshin wrote an article titled "Gandhi in the Eyes of Soviet Scholars" in a Russian journal which was later published in its English translation by the *Mainstream*.[61] He traced in it the evolution of Soviet ideas on Gandhiji and Gandhism. He writes: "Gandhi was too complicated a person to judge. He was a strong and unique personality capable of obeying his inner voice and disregarding the opinion of others." And then it was all the more difficult to do so from afar, in almost complete isolation from India. He further says: "India's national movement knew its ups and downs, offensives and retreats. . . . Gandhi's tactical deviations were taken as the essence of his position and gave rise to hasty and artificial conclusions not only among the Soviet scholars."

He refers to the view of M.N. Roy expressed in his book *India in Transition* and says: "In that period not only Roy and Nehru but also aspiring Swarajists severely criticized Gandhi."

But his own view is: "Gandhi was not a reactionary in the Indian National Congress. He was simply more farsighted than others and saw that the non-cooperation and civil resistance movement had been defeated and should be ended in order to preserve the leading role of the Indian National Congress."

He points out to the opinion of Lenin as against that of Roy and says: "Lenin believed that Gandhi, the inspirer and leader of the mass-scale movement, was a revolutionary, while Roy overemphasized his religious and cultural approach to social problems and considered him to be a reactionary, no matter how revolutionary his actions might seem from the political angle." However, he agrees with the view of Gandhi, as expressed in the big Soviet Encyclopaedia of 1929, being an exponent of petit-bourgeois ideology, but he says: "This basically correct view was, nevertheless, marked by two gross miscalculations. Firstly, it exaggerated the individualistic character of Gandhi's world outlook, and consequently disregarded his organic links with the widest sections of the nationalist movement, both in town and country. . . . Secondly, the absolutisation of the peasant aspect of Gandhism overshadowed the possibility of that ideology's use by the national bourgeoisie. . . . Hence the naive attempts to pass Gandhism as an ideology with no class roots in Indian society."

He finds fault with the Sixth Congress of Communist International which adopted a policy in which Lenin's theses on the unity of anti-imperialist forces were underestimated and the national bourgeoisie was proclaimed a counter-revolutionary force and an ally of imperialism. He later refers to the drastic change of view in 1956 and says: "The concept of Gandhism as a bourgeois ideology also began to be demolished. Gandhism was now presented as an anti-imperialist ideology with great democratic and national content."

He finds two estimates of the Gandhian ideal in the contemporary Soviet literature. Some look upon it as egalitarian while the other sees in it a version of peasant socialism. He is for the latter view and says: "Gandhi's *Sarvodaya* is a profound national and unique expression of the Utopian peasant ideal of socialism, but without elements of revolutionary democratism because of its devotion to non-violence." He, however, supports the view of some Soviet scholars that "*Sarvodaya* should not be confused with the bourgeois concept of welfare state. *Sarvodaya* aims at establishing public ownership of the means of production and abolishing exploitation of class by class, caste by caste and man by man."

He shows a better appreciation of the Gandhian trusteeship which has been an anathema to Indian Marxists. He accords it its due among the Gandhian methods of social transformation. He writes: "For all his anarchism, Gandhi being a political realist, could not overlook the vast potentialities of the state for transforming society. . . . He invested the state with important social and economic functions; specifically it was to control the exercise of trusteeship; determine remuneration for the trustees; appoint beneficiaries; even confiscate the property of landowners and capitalists if they failed to perform the duties of trustees and redistribute wealth through taxation." He points out that "To be able to give an unbiased opinion of Gandhi, it is essential to find the correct relationship between the two aspects of his being; political and moral, social and spiritual." And he further says: "It is pointless to argue which are more important for him — his search for truth or the social and political aims he pursued. It is essential (to point out) that his yearning for truth brought him to social and political activity which he regarded as an indispensable condition for moral growth. Herein lies the essence of his life and teaching, which made him a *Mahatma*".

He then deals with the international importance of nonviolence. He writes: "There is yet another aspect of Gandhi's heritage which invariably draws the attention of Soviet scholars. It is his humanitarian idea of nonviolence as adopted in international relations. He was an irreconcilable enemy of war. Hiroshima was for him an event that has confronted mankind with the choice of either starting disarmament immediately or perishing." He then refers to Gandhiji's article "Atom Bomb and Ahimsa" and says: "Whatever our attitude to his philosophy of non-violence may be, we cannot deny that his prestige as a leader of the Indian liberation movement served and continues to serve the cause of peace and disarmament. The Delhi Declaration between the Indian and Soviet leaders symbolizes the general human value of the principle of non-violence in international affairs. Although not a single state leader can fully share Mahatma's attitude to non violence, the proclamation of the principle of a world free from nuclear weapons unquestionably corresponds to the ideal Gandhi sought to attain."

Thus the Russian thinking of today may be said to have a better appreciation of the leadership role of Gandhiji and the relevancy of his nonviolence in international affairs. It is a step in right direction and, sooner or later, it may also see virtue in his other ideas as well.

NOTES AND REFERENCES

1. B.R. Nanda, *Mahatma Gandhi: A Biography* (Unwin Books, London, 1965), p. 26.
2. B.R. Nanda, *Socialism in India* (Vikas Publishing House, Delhi, 1972), p. 2.
3. P.C. Roy Chaudhury (ed.), *Gandhiji and Internal Politics* (Navajivan Publishing House, Ahmedabad, 1970), pp. 288 and 290-91.
4. B.R. Nanda, op cit., p. 3.
5. M.R. Masani, *The Communist Party of India: A Short History* (Bharatiya Vidya Bhavan, Bombay, 1967), p. 13.
6. D.G. Tendulkar, *Mahatma*, Vol. II (Publications Division, Govt. of India, Delhi, 1961), p. 254.
7. ibid, pp. 333-34.
8. Cited by Rafiq Zakaria in *Gandhi, Nehru and Russians*, in *Sunday Review* of *The Times of India*, September 30, 1984.
9. Ajit Bhattacharjee, *Jayaprakash Narayan: A Biography* (Vikas Publishing House, New Delhi, 1975), p. 78. Chapter Six of the book titled *The Communist Betrayal* deals with it.
10. "Gandhi and the Communists" in Sibnarayan Ray (Ed.), *Gandhi, India and the World* (Nachiketa Publications, Bombay, 1970), p. 206.
11. *Mao Tse-Tung and Gandhi* (Allied Publishers, Bombay, 1973), p. 18.
12. Nirmal Kumar Bose, *Selections from Gandhi* (Navajivan Publishing House, Ahmedabad, 1948), p. 3.
13. ibid.
14. ibid, p. 21.
15. G. Ramachandra Rao, *An Atheist with Gandhi* (Navajivan Publishing House, Ahmedabad, 1958), p. 31.
16. Nirmal Kumar Bose, op. cit, p. 223.
17. B.R. Nanda, *Gandhi and Religion* (Gandhi Smriti, New Delhi, n.d.), p. 5.
18. Nirmal Kumar Bose, op. cit, p. 93.
19. ibid, p. 92.
20. ibid, p. 96. For a fuller discussion on trusteeship see the Appendix.
21. Francis W. Coker, *Recent Political Thought* (D. Appleton-Century Company, New York, 1934), Chapter II dealing with Karl Marx.
22. ibid, pp. 164-65
23. Nirmal Kumar Bose, op. cit., p. 42.

24. ibid, p. 41.
25. Gopi Nath Dhawan, *The Political Philosophy of Mahatma Gandhi* (Navajivan Publishing House, Ahmedabad, 1962), p. 283.
26. J.B. Kripalani, *Gandhi: His Life and Thought* (Publications Division, Govt. of India, New Delhi, 1970), pp. 321-22.
27. ibid, pp. 404-05.
28. Gopi Nath Dhawan, op cit., pp. 207-08.
29. D.G. Tendulkar, *Mahatma*, Vol. VII, p. 29.
30. This aspect of Marx's thought has been dealt with in Francis W. Coker, op. cit., pp. 56-60.
31. Nirmal Kumar Bose, op cit., pp. 36 and 35.
32. ibid, p. 22-23.
33. ibid, pp. 22-23. Chandrashankar Shukla names it as "spiritual interpretation of history" in his *Gandhi's View of Life* (Bharatiya Vidya Bhavan, Bombay, 1956), Chapter XI.
34. Chandrashankar Shukla, op cit., p. 99 and Pyarelal, *The Last Phase*, Vol. II (Navajivan Publishing House, Ahmedabad, 1958), pp. 136-39. The letter to Carl Heath has been given by Shukla on p. 109 of his book.
35. Chandrashankar Shukla, op. cit., p. 83 and Pyarelal, op. cit., p. 139.
36. Pyarelal, op cit., pp. 136-37.
37. Tendulkar, *Mahatma*, Vol. VIII, pp. 8-9.
38. ibid, p. 9.
39. Gene D. Overstreet and Marshall Windmiller, *Communism in India* (University of California Press, 1959), p. 515.
40. ibid, pp. 515-16.
41. ibid, p. 516.
42. E.M.S. Namboodiripad, *The Mahatma and the Isms* (People's Publishing House, New Delhi, 1958), p. 111.
43. ibid, p. 112.
44. ibid, pp. 118-19.
45. Overstreet and Windmiller, op. cit, p. 518.
46. ibid, p. 521.
47. *The Mahatma: Marxist Evaluation* (People's Publishing House, New Delhi, 1977), pp. 5-6.
48. ibid, pp. 32-33 and 36.
49. ibid, p. 48.
50. ibid, pp. 65 and 68.
51. ibid, p. 90.
52. ibid, The opinion of Spratt about Gandhiji's attitude towards

communists has been cited above. Sardesai, however, says about it that though Gandhiji never called for or justified measures against Communists, and always approached Indian Communists as dedicated though erring youngsters, he fully reciprocated their basic antipathy towards Marxism, towards the very concept of class struggle and hence towards them (p. 46).

53. ibid, p. 90.
54. Cited in Sharad Patil, *EMS on Nationalism and Socialism* in the *Mainstream* of May 20, 1989.
55. ibid.
56. ibid.
57. Rafiq Zakaria, op. cit.
58. Communist opposition to Gandhi's plea for trusteeship has been already indicated above. A discussion of it will be found in the Appendix.
59. J.D. Sethi, *Impact of Gandhian Idea on Gorbachev* in the *Mainstream* of August 13, 1988.
60. ibid.
61. *Mainstream*, January 26, 1988.

CHAPTER TWO
Vinoba and Marx

"What can be a more fascinating study to us in the present age than that of a comparison between the ideologies of Gandhi, the great soul *(mahatma)*, and Marx, the great thinker *(mahamuni)*? If the last hundred years of the social life of humanity were boiled away, the residue will, most likely be these two names." That was observed by Vinoba in 1951 in his Introduction to K.G. Mashruwala's *Gandhi and Marx*. He also wrote in it that the two ideologies "are irreconcilable, the differences between them are fundamental".[1] He, however, did not mean by this that there could be no cooperation between them, for he said in 1957: "There can be no compromise between Sarvodaya and communism, though they can cooperate a great deal."[2] All these ideas of Vinoba were based on his study and deep thinking.

STUDY OF MARXISM

Gandhiji studied Marx during his detention in the Aga Khan Palace at Pune for his Quit India demand of 1942. This delay is understandable. The ideas of Marx caught world wide attention only after the successful Russian Revolution of 1917 when a State based on his ideas had come into existence. By that time the basic ideas of Gandhiji had evolved, and soon after he got so much involved in the freedom movement as to be left with little time to study Marx, even if he had a will for it. But with Vinoba it was different. Born in 1895 and given to study by nature, he studied *Das Kapital* at some time probably in the 1930s. This study combined with the extracts read out to him by a Marxist fellow prisoner while he was in jail for participation in the Individual Satyagraha of 1940, gave him the impression that the Marxist literature "deep in some places and shallow in others, is as wide and shoreless as the sea"[3], and that communism has at its back the support of a scientific terminology. But he did not consider it worthy of any critical examination since it was to him "obviously an ideology of attachment".[4]

However, a study of Vinoba's speeches and writings shows that he had begun expressing his ideas on Marxism, which he identified with 'communism', as early as December 1941, when in two of his lectures delivered in public, he touched upon it. In one of them he explained *dialectic* in an easily comprehensible language, and applying it to the nonviolent resistance of Gandhiji declared its superiority as a *synthesis*. He also said then that "just as the third element of *synthesis* is born by itself, the method of (nonviolent) resistance occurred to Gandhi because of the conditions in India." To cite his own words: "The sages too get their ideas and inspiration from (prevailing) conditions. The idea which occurred to Gandhi undoubtedly points to a special quality of his mind, but the real cause of its discovery lay in Indian conditions."[5]

The second speech indicated Vinoba's spirit of eclecticism, his open-mindedness and readiness to accept truths in other viewpoints. He said: "There is no ism devoid of merit. If we discard the good points of any ism, declaring it to be completely distorted, the ism acquires vitality. . . No ism loses its validity by simply looking at its shortcomings." Another significant observation of his on this occasion, though not directly related to Marxism, was: "In the field of science experiments are done in laboratories. If a theory is established, it finds a wider application and is made use of in society. The power of steam was discovered in an individual's experiments. . . . It was later used in society. Had that experiment remained confined to that person only, it would not have served any purpose. The power of nonviolence works even if confined to an individual."[6]

Some reflections on communism are also there in Vinoba's *Swaraj Sastra*, first published in Marathi in 1942. They would be referred to at appropriate places. However, the most important from this viewpoint is his "Introduction" to Mashruwala's book, referred to previously. He probably dealt with Marxism at some length in it because after independence the country had to decide about the path and model for its development. Some Gandhians even then were being attracted by the Chinese example and Vinoba felt the necessity of clarifying the similarities and differences between the two thoughts.

Vinoba's ideas were further developed and clarified during the Bhoodan-Gramdan movement, when communist workers and intellectuals under Marxian influence used to meet and discuss ideas and programmes with him. These are interspersed in his literature, though some important ones of them have been compiled under the title of *Sarvodaya aur Samyavad* in Hindi. This study tries to deal with the ideas of Vinoba somewhat systematically.

ATTITUDE TOWARDS MARX

Vinoba, as already indicated, had a great respect for Marx, the thinker, and accepted that communism has the support of a scientific terminology. But on the basis of Marx's well-known statement that "all I know is that I am not a Marxist", uttered in a moment of irritation at the misinterpretation of his doctrine concerning history, Vinoba felt that had he been alive today, he would have rewritten *Das Kapital*. It was not possible for him at that time to have foreseen the vast changes brought about now by science and technology.[7] Despite all this, Vinoba was unable to reconcile himself with the thinking of Marx. But before dealing with this aspect of Vinoba's thinking, it would be better to examine the strong points he found in Marxism or communism.

MERIT OF MARXISM

In his 1941 lecture which exhibited his eclecticism, Vinoba had pointed out that communism reposes faith in the poor to the highest degree. In *Swaraj Sastra* he found communism more attractive than fascism and he said in 1955: "I have been of the view that communism is a noble and broad-minded ideology, superior to capitalism in every way."[8] Further, in a conversation with a communist in 1964, his first preference was for the path of Sarvodaya and second for that of communism, considering it to be better than the *status quo*.[9] This statement of his must be construed in the same light as that of Gandhiji when preferred violence to cowardice. Vinoba also held that notwithstanding all its military strength, capitalism would not be able to meet the challenge of communism, because of its lack of sympathy for the suppressed and the oppressed. He also had no dislike for the communists since they were inspired by compassion, though he found them obsessed by a desire for immediate results, and he compared their intense love for the poor with that of a mother who lacked necessary discernment.[10] He refuted the idea that communists were destructionists and praised communism as an ideology which favours rational thinking, a quality not observed in earlier ideologies.[11] Vinoba also commended the Marxian ideal of the 'withering away of the state'. He held that as long as there is an order imposed from above, people would remain suppressed and would have no opportunity for free development.[12]

GENERAL CRITICISM OF MARXISM

Vinoba's objections against Marxism may, for systematic treatment, be divided into two parts — general criticism and criticism of important ideas. I deal here with general objections first.

The first shortcoming of Marxism, according to Vinoba, is that it is not a complete and independent ideology. It is a reaction to capitalism and therefore it is an *antithesis*. The result is that it is continually undergoing changes and does not have that stability which it should have. That is why the Russian communism is not the communism envisaged by Marx in his writings. Stalin departed from the policies of Lenin, Chinese communism differs from that of Russia, and the Indian communists agreed to work under the Indian Constitution.[13] Moreover, there is always a tendency in a thought born of reaction to acquire many defects of the original.[14] Vinoba wrote in *Swaraj Sastra*: "Within the short space of twenty years, the Russian Revolution has become so colourless that it has almost lost all its attractiveness. The reason for this is that of the four aspects of capitalism — centralization, large-scale machinery, militarism and exploitation — Socialism (communism) seeks to retain the first three and to do without the last. But such an attempt is based on delusion."[15]

The second shortcoming is that Marxism does not believe in the existence of soul and hence accords primacy to the physical body, when, in reality, the human level is a higher level and the man is something different from his physical body. Consequently, the very basis of equality so staunchly advocated by Marxism is knocked out and it is compelled to impose an artificial equality from above by violence.[16] Further, in a soulless ideology the individual has no importance and the question of individual liberty becomes irrelevant. It is only society which matters, for it is something enduring.[17]

Thirdly, the communists are not interested in devising a technique in accord with a true philosophy. They are, on the contrary, out to manufacture and trim a philosophy to suit their technique.[18] An illustration of it would be their pronouncement that all rules of ethics are relative and reflect the class character of society. This led them to neglect the intimate relationship subsisting between ends and means, and consequently to the adoption of violence, when violence can never be the power of the people. It is due to it that the Russian experiment failed to materialize into a rule of the many and turned out to be a rule by the few.[19]

Fourthly, Marxism preaches envy of the 'haves', when the so-called 'haves' have nothing to be envied for and such envy can lead nowhere.[20]

Lastly, there is no valid place for suffering and sacrifice in Marxism. In the words of Vinoba: "Though they (communists) make a lot of sacrifice, go to the people and live a life of poverty like them, there is no place for it in their philosophy."[21]

CRITICISM OF IMPORTANT IDEAS

Before beginning the criticism of the particular ideas of Marx, it must be pointed out that Marx has been variously interpreted, and there is no one Marx. Due to the achievements of Lenin, his interpretation naturally appealed to many and Leninism became synonymous with Marxism. However, the ideology of Russian communism itself has been changing from time to time. Stalin's interpretation of Marxism-Leninism held sway at one time, though he is universally accused now of deviating from Lenin and distorting Marxism-Leninism by his personality cult. With his death in 1953, and specially after the 20th Congress in 1956, Russian Marxism entered a new phase with some appreciation and accommodation for other viewpoints. But for most of the period during which Vinoba had been voicing his criticism energetically, it were the ideas of Stalin which had been dominating Marxism, and it is with reference to them that Vinoba's criticism must be taken as primarily directed, though it applies, with somewhat less vehemence, to the present-day communism as well.

Now as regards the criticism proper, the various ideas are being dealt with below one by one:

(a) *Dialectical Materialism:* Dialectical materialism forms the basis of Marxian philosophy. As Stalin said, its approach to phenomena of nature, its method of studying and apprehending them is dialectical, while its interpretation, its conception of the phenomena of nature is materialistic. According to it, everything is in a state of flux, and the development proceeds, due to internal contradictions, through the triads of *thesis*, *antithesis*, and *synthesis*. All change has a quantitative aspect, but as it proceeds further, it results in a qualitative change at a certain point and this qualitative change takes place relatively by a leap.

To Vinoba, *dialectic* was simply a logical tool. He did not think that the conclusions derived by Marx with the aid of dialectic were the only ones that could be arrived at. He said: "I could not understand how this theory creates a zeal for revolution and how it follows from it that 'haves' must be extirpated".[22] He was also of the opinion that it was not the only way of evolution. Some changes are intentional and results of rational considerations.[23]

He, however, agreed with Marx on two points. First, he also held that human society has been evolving, albeit in the direction of nonviolence; and, secondly, there were leaps in the process, quantitative changes leading to qualitative changes which occur suddenly.[24] However, Vinoba was not happy at the use of the word 'materialism', which is also taken to stand for Epicureanism.[25]

(b) *Materialistic Interpretation of History:* This interpretation of history is an application of dialectical materialism to human society. According to it, the clue to the development of human society does not lie in intellectual and moral factors but in the practical methods of production and the physical and cultural conditions of production which create certain relations of production, and it is these relations that chiefly determine the whole cultural order of an epoch — its moral, religious, social, and political institutions and ideas. The cultural order constitutes a superstructure based on the substructure of the economic factors mentioned previously. Marx held that the superstructure reflects the material interests of the dominating class in society. The argument advanced in favour of this view is that the material conditions of the life of society of which the foremost is the production of material values are primary, while the views of the people, their ideas and theories are secondary.[26] In other words, man has to live first, and thinking comes later.

Vinoba, while not denying that man has to live first,[27] could not accept Marx's interpretation of history with its corollary that societal change needed first change in the social structure of society. According to him, the two fundamental creeds, one giving primacy to the change in man for change in society and the other according primacy to change of social conditions, are very old, and in between them have been lying other views, some inclined on one side and others on the other side. Gandhiji, Vinoba said, did not deny the importance of change in the social structure but he held that it should be brought about only through the development of the necessary moral attributes. There were certain abiding moral values and norms, and if they were lost in a hurry in somehow setting up a particular social structure, it would tantamount to losing the capital in an avaricious bid for interest. In other words, Gandhiji held that it was truer to say that a good social structure could be achieved only when there was adequate moral development.[28] And Vinoba subscribes to this very view. Once asked whether revolution required change in the individual society, his reply was that both had their place. To insist on one only would be wrong, a *duragraha*. There should be elasticity in our ideas. He, however, gave primacy to man.[29]

Vinoba's criterion to measure the progress of a society is different from that of the Marxists. The latter would judge a society by its economic affluence as shared by all. According to a Russian publication, "in order to judge how far the whole of society and not its individual spheres have developed, we need a definite criterion. Such a criterion is, first and foremost, the level of development of the productive forces in unity with the relations of production."[30] For Vinoba the main touchstone was how far the members of a society had transcended their physical self and developed compassion.[31]

An aspect of Marx's interpretation of history is also his conception of revolution and its process. Marx's idea of a revolution was that of a social one and the same was true of Vinoba. Thus both stood for a total change in society. But they differed as to the process. Since Marx accorded primacy to the change in social structure, for him the road to it lay through the seizure of power. In the words of Lenin, "the question of power is the fundamental question of every revolution."[32] Vinoba, on the contrary, did not attach much importance to it. He did not believe that power could bring about basic changes in society. He had argued that Buddha, Christ, and Gandhiji wrought revolutions but they never worshipped power.[33]

To Vinoba, a revolution meant a change of heart, a change in values. According to him, the three sides of a triangle of a revolution were the change of ideas, the change of life and the change in society. He once said that all revolutions, social or economic, have their roots in spiritual ideas. The first to undergo change are spiritual values and then follow changes in social, economic and political values. Vinoba had great faith in the potentiality of thought and found its proof in the communists themselves.[34]

In the context of the process of revolution an important question which arises concerns the role of an individual. The Marxists do not completely deny him a role, but they do belittle it. Vinoba attaches much greater importance to it. He once pointed out that Buddha, Christ and Muhammad provide proof that revolutionary ideas are first born in the minds and hearts of individuals.[35] He also held theoretically like Gandhiji that if there were a single individual of complete purity, he would be able to bring about a revolution. But he admitted that the ideas of an individual would only be acceptable to society if they answered some need of the age. In the beginning a few would act upon them, then some groups and finally the society would accept them.[36]

(c) *Class Struggle:* The *Communist Mainfesto* declared: "The history of all existing societies is the history of class struggles." Thus, according to Marx, class struggle is the driving force which makes a society move onward. He held that it would ultimately result in the liberation of man, and hence the Marxist strategy for societal change has been to intensify class feelings and thereby the class struggle. Vinoba rejected the very idea of the division of men into classes — the 'haves' and the 'have-nots'. He argued that if there were some people economically rich, the others too were rich in their capacity to do labour.[37] He characterized the class perspective as a 'jaundiced vision.' He held that the world runs not on conflict but on love.[38]

To the communist charge that the Gandhians stood for class collaboration and not for class abolition, Vinoba's reply was that they too wanted to do away with classes but it could not be achieved through waging class struggle, which would only strengthen class feelings and, in the Indian context, caste feelings. Therefore what was really required was not a programme of friction but of churning. The former produces heat while the latter produces butter. The idea of struggle was a Western conception, injurious in every way. Class struggle would never lead to peace in society. As a violent method it would result in counterviolence, and both would depreciate human values.[39] His advice for attaining a classless society was that "some ten or twenty of us known to each other should join together, equally distribute our wealth and successfully demonstrate in our own lives the experiments of a classless social structure."[40]

(d) *The State:* Marx deemed the State as a part of the superstructure built on the substructure of its economic relations to protect the interests of the dominant class. Lenin wrote in his *State and Revolution*: "According to Marx, the state is an organ of class domination, an organ of oppression of one class by another; its aim is the creation of 'order' which legalises and perpetuates this oppression by moderating the collisions between the classes...." Gandhiji thought differently, even though he considered State to represent violence in a concentrated and organised form, a soulless machine which could never be weaned away from violence.[41]

Vinoba's thinking, though not opposed to that of Gandhiji, was somewhat independent in exposition. Despite his advocacy of a government-free society, his attitude towards the State appeared to be more accommodating in that he was not prepared to place the penal power of the State at par with violence, and held that under the existing situation such penal power has a place in society. In his nonviolent society, the most important institution would be a service institution. The penal power would be there, but used rarely. At the same time, he opined that the worst disease afflicting the world these days was the State. There was no real need of it and it had merely happened in history.[42]

The Marxian ideal of the withering away of the State commended itself to Vinoba since the Sarvodaya too shared it, but he could not agree that the path to it lay through the establishment of any dictatorship; even if it be the dictatorship of the proletariat. On the other hand, that ideal needed decentralization of administration and authority for its realization.[43]

(e) *Religion:* Gandhi was 'religious-minded' and so was

Vinoba, though their concept of religion significantly differed from the popular one. Marx, on the other hand rejected religion as an opiate of the people. He wrote: "Religion is the sigh of the hard-pressed creature, the heart of a heartless, the spirit of unspiritual condition. It is the opium of the people."[44] All this could not be acceptable to Vinoba, though he did not approve everything that passes for religion these days. He held that religion, if correctly understood, is conducive to the good of mankind. He once remarked: "There are many who pride in the name of religion, there are many who start trouble in the name of religion, but there are few who practise the essence of religion."[45] He found no grounds for conflict between science and religion, and even thought that the advance of science would not adversely affect such subtler ideas of religion as love, nonviolence, compassion, etc. At the same time, he felt that outer forms of religions needed change. He was opposed to organised religions and was of the view that state support leads to their decline.[46] Unlike Marx, he believed in God, who was more real to him than any material object. But he preferred honest atheists hundreds of thousand times to those theists who took the name of God but exploited men, and he held that sincere atheists were nearer to God than nominal theists.[47]

The fact is that Vinoba's perspective on religion was basically different from that of Marx. Marx's views were the outcome of his Western experiences, while Vinoba's had been influenced by Indian, or say Hindu, thought and culture. However, despite all communist condemnation of religion, the religious feelings are so ingrained in man that the communists have failed to liberate themselves from them. Some commentators had noted that Russian communism, despite its anti-religious professions and practices, has become religious in its prevailing mood, including the 'apotheosis' of Lenin.[48]

(f) *Morality:* Gandhian thought lays utmost stress on morality and regards cardinal principles like truth and nonviolence to be true for all times and peoples. The Marxists question it on the basis of their interpretation of history. It was said in the *Communist Manifesto*: "Law, morality, religion are to him (the labourer) so many bourgeois prejudices, behind which lurk in ambush just as many bourgeois interests." What the Marxists stand for is a 'real human morality', which, according to Engels, would transcend class antagonisms and their legacies in thought. But such a morality would be possible only when society would overcome not merely class antagonisms but would forget them in practical life. This morality would be characterized by a lack of dogmatism, and would be scientific and self-critical. It would consider immoral behaviour to be simply anti-social behaviour.[49]

Vinoba's approach to morality was different, though it was not opposed to the Marxist conception of human morality. Like Gandhiji, he did not think in terms of classes, not because class feelings, directly or indirectly, did not exist but because the individual was more important to him. Hence he looked upon social evils in terms of individuals. As regards the principles of morality, he divided them into two categories, relative and absolute. He once said that the prevailing notions of righteousness and unrighteousness are mostly conventional. Among the absolute principles, he placed truth, love, compassion, etc. He once said: "The observance of truth is as much a duty today as it was in days gone by, and as much in other countries as in India. The difference of time and space does not limit it. It belongs to the category of eternal verities, which are ever the same always. So are love and compassion.

But the rules of conduct through which they are sought to be expressed cannot last for all times. They change according to age, circumstances and country."[50] It may also be mentioned here that the present-day Marxian thought in Russia has indirectly begun to recognize that there are some universal elements in morality, though it still focuses attention on its class contents.[51]

(g) *Economic Ideas:* Marx's theory of surplus value was reckoned by Engels among his crowning theoretical discoveries. Marx had found in it an explanation for the misery of the proletariat and expected that increasing misery would ultimately result in a socialist revolution. But this surmise of his proved wrong. Vinoba was also among those who pointed to it.[52] But he never referred to the theory of surplus value, probably because he did not have that much of interest in economic theories.

Vinoba differed from Marx on the principles of the economic reconstruction of society. While Marx advocated economic centralization and, roughly speaking a rising standard of living, Vinoba, as is well-known, stood for economic decentralization, simplicity of life and area or regional self-sufficiency in the basic necessities of life. Both, however, advocated the principle of cooperation, but, unlike Marxists, Vinoba did not favour its imposition from above.[53]

It must also be mentioned here that Vinoba's concept of economic decentralization is marked by a sort of synthesis between the old non-centralization and the modern large-scale industrialism. He did not think modern industrialism to be totally devoid of virtues. He recognized that its purpose was to liberate man from unnecessary labour. Hence his economic decentralization attempted to incorporate the virtues of modern industrialism or, as he put it, the advantages of the machine age.[54]

(h) *Alienation:* The present-day sociological literature talks a great deal of the phenomenon of alienation, increasingly being observed in developed societies. This phenomenon has generally been explained as the alienation of men from their labour, alienation from the commodities they produce, alienation of consumption from production, alienation of man from social organization, and alienation of man from one another. To this some would even add alienation of man from nature, which in recent years is the theme of the science of ecology. Marx had pointed to alienation in his *Economic and Philosophical Manuscripts of 1844* and along with Ludwig Feuerbach, he is credited for secularization of the concept. However, the sociologists became aware of the phenomenon only in the 1930s to some extent and more widely after the Second World War, and in this the early writings of Marx played an important role.[55]

Marx, however, did not attribute it to modern industrialism. He held the economic system, i.e. the property system and especially the private ownership of production, responsible for it, and hence the remedy suggested by him was a communist reorganization of society. To neutralize the effects of the division of labour, which too contributes to alienation, he thought of job change, which even the Marxists of today do not think practicable.[56]

The fact is that in this context the ideas of Gandhiji are more relevant. B.N. Ganguli writes: "Gandhi's lifestyle bridged the gulf between the heart and the intellect, between claims of humanism, self-determination and freedom, on the one hand, and those of social and political organization, on the other."[57] That is probably why the thought of the New Left is reminiscent of Gandhiji's social philosophy.[58] It also tabes into account the alienation of man from nature, whose awareness is growing. And what is true of Gandhiji in this respect is still truer of Vinoba, who has, on the whole, clarified and applied Gandhiji's ideas in the context of present-day situation. However, neither of them ever directly referred to the phenomenon of alienation.

SAMYA-YOGA

A comparative study of the ideas of Marx and Vinoba has been presented above. Vinoba claimed that Sarvodaya was the only ideology which thought of all. He named his thinking *Samya-yoga* as against *Samya-vada*, the ideology of communism or Marxism. *Samya-yoga* believes that Spirit is equally immanent in all, and therefore all life is one and an inner unity runs through all. It is on the basis of this spiritual unity that *Samya-yoga* seeks to build up an equitable social order wherein everything shall have its rightful place. While *Samya-yoga* is opposed to inequality, it is not against right discrimination and hence it provides scope for development to every individual.[59]

These ideas led Vinoba to advocate a social structure similar to that of Gandhiji and to insist on the adoption of purest means for its attainment.

CONCLUSION

The above study of Vinoba's ideas in the context of Marxian ideas leads to the conclusion that they represent a sort of synthesis between Marxism and Western liberalism, enriched by an insight of Indian culture.

Much has been written for and against Marxian ideas and the debate would continue. What is more important is that thinkers all over the world are agreed that there is a substratum of truth in the ideas of Marx. Vinoba also recognizes it. Marx had once said: "The philosophers have only interpreted the world in various ways; the point is, to change it." Vinoba, like Gandhiji, was also interested in changing the world, but this change was not one-sided. It involved both outer and inner transformation. Marx did not, in words at least attach importance to the latter, and that is probably why Vinoba found Marxism shallow at some places.

A question often raised is if the ideology of Gandhiji and that of Marx can converge and unite to fight the common enemy of poverty and exploitation. This question was even posed by Romain Rolland.[60] The answer, that Vinoba gave and to which reference has already been made, was that the two can cooperate but there can be no ideological compromise between the two. There are many matters on which the two agree and these provide a field for cooperation. But here too there seems to be a stumbling block, and it relates to the purity of means. This would make cooperation more superficial than real. But it may be well hoped that with the passage of time the desirability of nonviolence and of the purity of means will be increasingly recognized, and then there may be real cooperation. However, many Sarvodayites in India look upon the communists with suspicion both on account of the transitional society envisaged by them and the policies pursued by them. Vinoba, however, never lost faith in man, communist or non-communist.

NOTES AND REFERENCES

1. Introduction to K.G. Mashruwala, *Gandhi and Marx* (Ahmedabad, 1951).
2. *Bhoodan Yajna*, June 7, 1957.
3. Introduction to K.G. Mashruwala, *Gandhi and Marx*.
4. ibid.
5. This lecture is available in the Hindi collection of Vinoba, *Vinoba Ke Vichar* (Sasta Sahitya Mandal, New Delhi), Vol. II, pp. 86-95.
6. ibid., pp. 96-113.
7. *Bhoodan*, August 15, 1958. Marx's statement and its circumstances have been mentioned in Peter Singer, *Marx* (Oxford, 1980), p. 38.
8. *Swaraj Sastra* (Padma Publications, Bombay, 1945) *Bhoodan Ganga*, Vol. IV (Varanasi, 1957), p. 43.
9. *Sarvodaya aur Samajavad* (Varanasi, July 1965), p. 85.
10. *Vinoba Pravachan*, January 12, 1963. K.G. Mashruwala, *Gandhi and Marx*, pp. 29-30.
11. *1957 Kaladi Sarvodaya Sammelan Proceedings* (Hindi), p. 71.
12. *Savodaya aur Samajavad*, p. 73.
13. ibid., p. 38.
14. *Vinoba Pravachan*, August 3, 1957.
15. ibid., p. 27-28.
16. *Harijan*, April 19, 1952.
17. Introduction to K.G. Mashruwala, *Gandhi and Marx*.
18. *Swaraj Sastra*, p. 20.
19. ibid.
20. *Sarvodaya aur Samajavad*, pp. 44-45.
21. ibid., p. 50.
22. ibid., pp. 40-41.
23. In a conversation with the author in 1950.
24. *Talks on the Gita* (Varanasi, 1959), pp. 234-38. See also *Bhoodan Yajna*, April 4, 1958.
25. *Sarvodaya aur Samajavad*, p. 40.
26. G. Glegarman and G. Kursanov (eds.), *Historical Materialism* (Moscow, 1968), p. 19 and 103.
27. Vinoba, like Gandhi, held that to a poor person God must first appear in the orm of food. He had often quoted the example of Buddha who advised his disciples to serve food first to a starving person, and preach later.
28. Introduction to K.G. Mashruwala, *Gandhi and Marx*.

29. *Sarvodaya* (Hindi), April-May 1955, Appendix; *Krant Darshan* (Varanasi, 1962), p. 132.
30. V. Paodosetnike and A. Spirikin, *A Glance at Historical Materialism* (Moscow, n. d.), pp. 130-31.
31. *Bhoodan*, July 11, 1956.
32. Cited in Maurice Cornforth, *Dialectical Materialism* (Calcutta, 1954), Vol. II, p. 87.
33. *Prarthana Pravachan*, July 19, 1957; *Harijan Sevak*, June 26, 1949.
34. *Sarvodaya*, July 1949, p. 696; *Vinoba Pravachan*, July 11, 1957; and *Bhoodan Yajna Bihar*, 1-3, p. 5.
35. *Bhoodan*, May 29, 1957.
36. *Bhoodan Yajna Bihar*, November 6, 1953 and June 12, 1953.
37. *Sarvodaya*, July 1953, p. 796.
38. Introduction to K.G. Mashruwala, *Gandhi and Marx*; *Swaraj Sastra*, pp. 14-15; and *Harijan*, December 6, 1952.
39. Vishwanath Tandon, ed., *Selections from Vinoba* (Varanasi, 1981), pp. 101-102. Its second edition has been published by National Gandhi Museum, New Delhi in 2004.
40. *Sarvodaya* (Hindi), December 1949, p. 293.
41. Nirmal Kumar Bose (ed.), *Selections from Gandhi* (Ahmedabad, 1948), p. 42.
42. *Bhoodan Ganga*, Vol. III p. 203; *Sarvodaya* (Hindi), April-June 1955, p. 602: and Vinoba, *Lokniti* (Varanasi, 1959), pp. 81-82. There is some contradiction involved in the statements here, but it is inevitable when some statements reflect realism, while others reflect idealism. It is also observed in the statements of Gandhi.
43. Vinoba Bhave, *Democratic Values* (Varanasi, 1962), p. 29.
44. Cited in Caudwel, *Further Studies in a Dying Culture* (London, 1950), p. 75.
45. *Prarthana Pravachan*, May 28, 1957.
46. Vishwanath Tandon, *Selections from Vinoba*, pp. 28-30; *Bhoodan*, 27 February 1957; *Vinoba Pravachan*, November 10, 1957; and *Democratic Values*, p. 18.
47. Vinoba, *Random Reflections* (Varanasi, 1957), p. 233; *Vinoba Pravachan*, June 2, 1959.
48. F.W. Coker, *Recent Political Thought* (New York, 1934), p. 179.
49. Maurice Cornforlh, *Historical Materialism*, Vol. III, pp. 258-59.
50. *Prarthana Pravachan*, April 29, 1957; *Harijan*, December 20, 1952; *Bhoodan Yajna Bihar,* July 24, 1953; *Vinoba Chintan*, No. 7, p. 31.
51. G. Glegarman and G. Kursanov, *Dialectical Materialism*, p. 290.

52. *Sarvodaya aur Samajavad*, p. 37.
53. *Swaraj Sastra*, p. 45.
54. *Harijan*, December 20, 1952.
55. Article on *Alienation* in *Encyclopaedia Britannica* (*Micropaedia*), 1982 edn.
56. ibid. See also Milkos Almasi, *Alienation and Socialism* in Herbert Apthekar (ed.), *Marxism and Alienation* (New York, 1965), p. 131.
57. B.N. Ganguli, *Gandhi's Social Philosophy* (Vikas, New Delhi, 1973), p. 387. The book has been reprinted by National Gandhi Museum in 2000.
58. ibid., p. 382.
59. *Harijan*, November 7, 1953 and April 19, 1952.
60. B.N. Ganguli, *Gandhi's Social Philosophy*, pp. 356-57.

CHAPTER THREE

Marxists and Vinoba

The Telangana struggle which had been responsible for the birth of the Bhoodan movement, had brought Vinoba in somewhat close contact with the communists of the region when he tried to win them over to the path of nonviolence. This contact and the subsequent flowering of the movement into Gramdan movement which had a greater appeal for the communists, compelled them and their fellow thinkers to pay greater attention to the movement, to study it and to define their attitude towards it. This compelled some prominent communist Marxists to express their views on some important ideas of Vinoba and his movement. But it was not all. They had been highly critical of the ideas of Gandhiji which, in the post-Independence period, were being creatively interpreted and applied by Vinoba. Therefore their criticism and appraisal of Gandhiji were relevant to Vinoba as well. Hence for a complete picture of their attitude towards Vinoba, one has to study both of these materials and it would be more conducive to understanding to take up first their attitude towards Gandhiji.

ATTITUDE TOWARDS GANDHIJI

Gandhiji had been an enigma to the communists during his lifetime. They could neither accept his leadership nor denounce it totally. The main cause of it was the presence of the two elements of anti-capitalism and anti-colonialism in the international communist movement, which were not always in complete accord. Sometime the former predominated and, at other times, the latter, During the first period, Gandhiji with his religious attitude, his emphasis on nonviolence and purity of means, his plea for an agrarian society, and values of life, his advocacy of trusteeship, etc., was denounced as a 'bourgeois' leader, but during the period when support to anti-colonialism seemed necessary for their own purpose, the freedom struggle under Gandhiji acquired a different character, deserving support and participation. However, it was for the purpose of influencing it and bringing it closer to their ideology. Admitting it, S.G. Sardesai says: "After all, the fundamental purpose of our efforts to understand Gandhi and his role in the national movement was to establish such relations with the mass movement led by him as would enable us to shatter its ideological integument and carry forward the millions under Gandhi's influence to genuine revolutionary action."[1] But they succeeded in their objective very inadequately and partially, and this because "Gandhi always eluded our efforts to grapple with his ideas and policies."[2] Sardesai's explanation for it is: "The mistake lay in the immature, lopsided and over-simplified understanding of the task by the CPI: the mistake lay in the failure to grasp the complexities of the task to which it had been called by history. And here lies the meaning and explanation of Gandhi having proved an enigma for the CPI."[3]

Another reason for the failure of the CPI, which it would be too much to expect of any communist theoretician to mention, was that their thinking instead of being influenced by the objective conditions of India was determined by ideas from outside. And herein also lies the explanation of another admission of theirs that with "all his medieval social theories which in the contemporary context were theories of class collaboration, Gandhi knew and understood India better than we."[4]

The Communists, however, were compelled after independence, by national and international conditions, to review and adjust their judgement of Gandhiji, and this brought about some balance in their estimate of Gandhiji and his leadership. Vinoba, as will be seen later, reaped the benefit of this change in attitude. This change as circumstances would have it, synchronised with the first decade of the Bhoodan movement.

VIEWS ON VINOBA AND HIS MOVEMENT

Just as in the case of Gandhiji, communists' views on Vinoba also underwent changes with time. In the beginning they were suspicious of the Bhoodan movement. In an article published in 1953 in the CPI organ, *New Age*, P. Ramamurti wrote about the movement that "It was no movement of the people. It is charity — charity in land — just like charity for any other purpose."[5] He concluded from the speeches of Vinoba and others that "their primary and main aim is not the solution of the land problem, but preventing the strengthening of the development of the organisation and struggle of the peasant masses for their just demand."[6] A little later another note added to it was that the emergence of Vinoba Bhave was being watched with eagerness and expectation in the American camp and that the American lobby paid homage to the new 'messiah'. It also pointed out that the Bhoodan 'stunt' was basically reactionary in character and said, "It was being brought forward at a time when the shining example of the emancipation of the Chinese brother strikes deep chord in the heart of the Indian peasant."[7]

This stance, however, began to change later when it began to dawn on the communists that Gandhian constructive workers were becoming disillusioned with the Congress and that mutual dissatisfaction between them was growing. This new attitude became all the more apparent when Vinoba entered Kerala in his Bhoodan trek and expressed his opinion that Communists were no destructionists.[8] By this time the movement too had got converted into a movement and consequently, E.M.S. Namboodiripad, then the Chief Minister of Kerala, wrote that Vinoba Bhave's objective was as revolutionary as any communist or socialist would have.[9]

However, differences persisted regarding the method and Namboodiripad could not accept the proposition that in Gramdan, Vinoba and his followers had discovered the only possible and correct solution for the social problems of the country. While he agreed that Vinoba's teachings would help in the process of socio-economic transformations, he held that these too could not be brought about without use of state machinery, and he further pointed out that big landlords had not responded to Vinoba's call for the abolition of private property in land.[10]

Similar was the view of another important communist leader, B.T. Ranadive. He wrote in 1958 that while Sarvodaya accepted the profound truth of communism regarding the disappearance of state, abolition of exploitation and the principle "from each according to his ability, to each according to his need", it lacks an understanding of the concrete material foundation to realize it. He found it attaching almost exclusive importance to the land problem, which he attributed to the undeveloped condition of the country. He also criticized the Sarvodayites for claiming exaggerated virtues for Bhoodan and its method and pronounced it a failure, since much of the land donated was uncultivable and evictions continued in spite of the movement.[11] This failure, according to Ranadive was inevitable, since the movement had by-passed the laws of social struggle and economic realities.[12]

Ranadive accepted the idea of Gramdan as sound but was critical of the exaggerated advantages claimed for it. He felt it would not be able to put a stop to village exploitation unless other means of production too were socially owned. He did not expect the Gramdan movement to acquire the character of a mass movement.[13] Vinoba seemed to him to be a person of undecided mind like the Arjuna of the *Gita*. He also held like Namboodiripad that any struggle for social change, violent or nonviolent, would have to take the form of a political struggle. The oppressed class must organize itself into a party to liberate itself. Abstention from politics favoured the ruling class.[14] Vinoba's attitude towards political parties, elections and decision by majority indicated his apolitical and anti-authoritarian stand, which could not be that of a revolutionary working class.[15] He was also critical of Vinoba claiming to follow Gandhiji since he had neglected the most important heritage of Gandhiji, namely his nonviolent resistance, which had made Gandhiji a great leader of the people.[16]

Despite all this criticism, Ranadive admitted that Vinoba had made city people aware of the land problem, thrown his might on the side of peace and had a passionate urge for social transformation. He welcomed Vinoda's criticism of the institution of private property and recognized his friendly feelings for the communists and his efforts to understand their standpoint.[17] He also had words of sympathy for the selfless workers with Vinoba and appreciated the sincerity behind his activities.[18]

Both Namboodiripad and Ranadive represented the thinking of the CPI(M) group in the CPI, though by that time there had been no split in the party. As against them, the thinking of Mohit Sen, another theoretician, represents the thinking of the other group. According to him, there were three Gandhian streams after the death of Gandhiji, and they were represented by Jawaharlal Nehru, Vinoba Bhave and C.Rajagopalachari.[19] Regarding the Sarvodaya movement, he says: "In many ways the Sarvodaya movement represented the efforts of the Gandhians to break loose from the capitalist class while simultaneously combating the working class. It represented the efforts of the peasantry to play an independent role in a condition where the state of the national bourgeoisie was developing capitalism in compromise with imperialism and in alliance with the landlords."[20]

Sen saw in Gramdan with its abolition of private property, the common cultivation of common land along with the equal distribution of produce and the organization of village handicrafts on a cooperative basis, a return to the old village community which formed the basis of the mode of production in Asian countries. But he also pointed out that there was no such worked out scheme for the industrial sector, though there was some talk of *sampattidan*.[21] Mohit Sen commended Vinoba for publicly praising the policies and the practices of the communist ministry in Kerala and for adopting a catholic and progressive attitude on such a controversial issue as how to resolve the conflict with China.[22]

He too, however, found the real tragedy of the Sarvodaya

movement to lie in its eschewing all forms of governmental action, and at the same time, abandoning any form of mass action. This was unlike Gandhiji, who, while stressing the importance of 'heart conversion', had followed his preaching and appeals by fasts, non-cooperation, hartals and other forms of civil disobedience.[23] The overall conclusion of Mohit Sen was that the Bhoodan-Gramdan movement was a colossal failure, the land donated was often either unfit for cultivation or was encumbered with litigation, and the donors were often small peasants who despaired of eking out a living on their utterly paltry plots. Insofar as the chief aim lay not in securing land for redistribution but in bringing about a veritable revolution in the psychology of landlords for a revolutionary change in power-relationship at the village level so as to provide a basis for a Gandhian reconstruction of the whole of the Indian polity and society, Mohit Sen's view was that the achievements were worse than negative.[24] It may be mentioned here in passing that this criticism of the nature of donated land also finds support in a statement of Miraben made in 1953, and it has also been referred to by some others.

Mohit Sen, however, acknowledged that the Sarvodaya movement attracted some idealists who refused to be lured by the possibilities of becoming ministers, and that it had within it some ardent people who had been disgusted with the capitalist path and who genuinely desired a revolutionary reconstruction of Indian society.[25]

All these four Marxist thinkers — Sardesai, Ranadive, Namboodiripad and Sen — were definitely connected with either the CPI or the CPI(M), but there are a few other Marxist intellectuals as well who have dealt with Vinoba and his movement. One of them is C.G. Shah,[26] who is much more critical and less appreciative of the ideas of Gandhiji and Vinoba. He differentiated between Bhoodan and Sampattidan. According to him, the former aimed at a redistribution of land, the basic means of production, in contrast to the latter which aimed at the redistribution of income, endorsing by implication capitalistic private property in the means of production and thus investing it with bourgeois class character. Sampattidan, as he viewed it, considered income from exploitation as immoral but not the exploitation itself.[27]

Shah was also critical that both Bhoodan and Sampattidan movements were restricted to the ethical reconstruction of the consciousness of primarily the wealthy classes.[28] He writes: "It is not the change of heart which supplies motif to capitalist charity and philanthropy. It is mostly craze for fame or conscious or unconscious class interests."[29] Hence he denounced the movements "as a chloroform to dull the spirit of revolt of the masses."[30] The movements, according to him, were foredoomed to failure since Gandhiji's own moral appeals for over two decades had failed to make capitalists accept trusteeship.[31] He also noted another defect in Vinoba's movement in that it had eschewed the Gandhian mass action of satyagraha along with the legislative method for its purpose. All this led Shah to hold that Vinoba's movement was capable of doing harm to the growing class struggle in the country and of sabotaging both mass and parliamentary struggles for securing relief for the masses.[32]

More recently, Buddhadeva Bhattacharyya, a Marxist intellectual, has endorsed the above view of Shah that the eschewing of mass action as well as of the legislative programme was bound to harm the struggle of the toiling people. He writes: "The single thread that runs through bhoodan, gramdan, and sampattidan is the abjuration of political struggle, avoidance of all conflict, including satyagraha, to realize a universal brotherhood of humanity changing the very basis of the existing corrupt social order. For Vinoba and Sarvadayites method is the main consideration. . . . Needless to say that neither the goal nor the social transformation will thus be achieved. It will only help to create illusion in the minds of the people about the efficacy of 'change of heart' of these worshippers of Mammon thereby emasculating the growing movement of the toiling people."[33]

However, despite the above criticisms, one may say that with time the attitude of the Marxists in general had softened towards Vinoba. They had become convinced of his sincerity and earnestness and had realized the value of the Bhoodan-Gramdan movement in arousing mass consciousness, though they continued to emphasize that for the realization of the very objectives of his movement in society some sort of political struggle for the capture of power was absolutely necessary along with the social struggle.[34]

GENERAL CRITICISM OF GANDHIAN IDEAS

In the above account of the Marxist attitude towards Vinoba, some references have been made to the criticism of his process of revolution, but the Marxist criticism is not confined to it alone. In their writings exceptions have also been taken to many other ideas as well. A difference, however, is that while Gandhiji's ideas have been dealt with in detail, that of Vinoba have only been touched upon with the exception of an exclusive article on him by Buddhadeva Bhattacharyya in a special issue of *Gandhi Marg* exclusively devoted to Vinoba on his first death anniversary.[35] The criticism mainly relates to the general outlook of Gandhiji and Vinoba – their stress on full adherence to nonviolence and purity of means under all circumstances, their theory of trusteeship, the economic order envisaged by them, and their attitude towards the state.

To take the criticism of the general outlook first, C.G. Shah finds the philosophy of Gandhism based upon religious and metaphysical prejudices, subjective illusions and unhistorical social and economic ideas, and consequently acting as a brake on the material and intellectual development of India. He characterizes it as an unscientific and anti-progressive social philosophy.[36] This view is seconded by others. Sardesai wrote: "Gandhi's theistic ideology and tenets expressed through his creed of truth, nonviolence, love, renunciation, the inner voice, change of heart, trusteeship, etc. were the expressions of India's socio-economic backwardness and superstition of the Indian masses. Hence they are antiquated and unscientific."[37] According to Mohit Sen, "The whole ideology of Gandhism can be represented as the ideological reflex of the ruined but rising rich peasants and his longing for the revival of the village community."[38] Buddhadeva Bhattacharyya looks upon the Gandhian ideology as non-scientific humanism. He writes: "As is well-known, Ruskin's *Unto This Last* cast a deep influence on Gandhi's thought. It may be mentioned here that a trend of humanism emerged on the European scene after the advent of the Industrial Revolution. Carlyle, Ruskin and others were prominent among those humanists. Tolstoyanism and Gandhism are the continuation of that trend. . . . They certainly roused the consciousness of the depressed humanity against the artificial complexities of capitalist civilization but lack of knowledge of the historical development and scientific understanding of the social dynamics blinded them to solution of the ills of modern civilization and the socio-economic basis upon which it stood and still stands today. . . . By their unscientific solution, though permeated with humanistic feelings, they sowed illusions in the minds of the people. The same can be said of the Sarvodayites."[39] In an earlier work relating to the evolution of the political philosophy of Gandhiji, Bhattacharyya had also expressed the view that Gandhiji had no concept of history in the Western sense. He was influenced by the concept of Indian philosophy that time has neither a beginning nor an end.[40] In its favour he cites Gandhiji himself who had once remarked, "A few thousand years are but a speck in the vast time circle."[41] He attributes Gandhiji's great patience and incorrigible optimism about the redemption of mankind to his faith in this eternal vast time scale.[42] Bhattacharyya further finds the limitation of Gandhiji to lie, apart from the subjective factor, in his contradictions which reflected the contradictions of the age, and says that Gandhiji's ideas mirrored the complexity of the Indian situation and the contradictions embedded in the process of Indian social development.[43] His was the voice of the nation.[44]

NONVIOLENCE AND THE PURITY OF MEANS

As regards nonviolence, C.G. Shah held that Gandhiji propounded the theory of class collaboration and exhorted the people to discard violence in their struggle for national liberation, considering violence and evil in itself and its use reprehensible in all situation.[45] Buddhadeva Bhattacharyya too is critical of Gandhiji for his insistence on nonviolence and he attributes it to his failure to differentiate between what is evil and what is morally wrong. He argues that Marxism does not advocate violence for its own sake. It is thrust upon the oppressed by the ruling class. Its intensity depends upon the intensity of repression.[46] S.A. Dange has questioned the validity of Gandhiji's insistence on nonviolence by pointing out that he himself did not repeat the mistake of Chauri Chaura, when he had withdrawn the movement because of the incidence of public violence.[47] Namboodiripad even raised the question if there was anything like an absolute morality with an unalterable way for its application. His own view is that there is no such thing, since Gandhiji's own attitude towards war had been changing from time to time and the mistake of Chauri Chaura was not repeated indicating that his truth and nonviolence were relative and not absolute.[48]

As for the insistence on the purity of means, it is clear from the above that being based on the twin principles or moral imperatives of truth and nonviolence, it does not have much appeal for them. Raghavan N. Iyer writes: "Gandhi seems to stand almost alone among social and political thinkers in the firm rejection of a rigid dichotomy between ends and means and in the moral preoccupation with the means to the extent that they, rather than the ends, provide the standard of reference."[49] And he further adds: "The doctrine that the end justifies the means does not even require any special justification for the Marxist who accepts no super-historic morality, no categorical imperative, religious or secular. Engels declared in his letter to Herson Triar in 1889 that "any means that leads to the aim suits me as a revolutionary, whether it is most violent or that which appears to be most peaceable'."[50] This may be taken as the general attitude of the Indian Marxists, though sometimes they are apologetic about it. This is well illustrated by the position taken up by Hiren Mukerjee. He writes that at the time of the *Communist Manifesto*, Marx and Engels were convinced that "the violent overthrow of the bourgeoisie lays the foundation for the sway of the proletariat". When Marx said in his *Kapital* (Vol. I) that "Force is the midwife of every old society pregnant with a new one", they obviously, saw no prospect either of a peaceful or a legal revolution, though they were always opposed to insurrectionism of the Blanqui type and to *coup d'etat* by minorities. Mukerjee also says that "While making this generalization, Marx and Engles never laid down an iron-clad dogma."[51] However, to buttress up the Marxist case he cites elsewhere Thomas Jefferson who had said in the context of the reign of terror in revolutionary France: "In the struggle which was necessary many guilty persons fell without the forms of Trial, and with them, some innocent. These I deplore as much as anybody and shall deplore some of them to the day of my death. But I deplore them as I should have done had they fallen in battle. It was necessary to use the arm of the people, a machine not quite blind as balls and bombs, but blind to a certain degree."[52] But Mukerjee also advises caution and writes: "It must, however, be borne in mind, by Marxists as well as by others, that the problem of means is a very serious matter, that much avoidable suffering and failure has been caused by lack of proper care in this regard, that our whole attention might be given to finding the most immediately effective means with the result that, the end being distant, the means might themselves turn out to be such as would damage or even wreck the ends originally sought. Every possible precaution must be taken in ensuring from the practical point of view, adoption of that course of action alone which would, in the circumstances prevailing, produce a balance of good results. . . . This is a moral choice of a kind which is extremely difficult and complicated, but it has to be made."[53]

TRUSTEESHIP

As to the principle of trusteeship, Buddhadeva Bhattacharyya cites a Marxist who says: "The division of society into the property-owning and propertyless classes, which is the characteristic of capitalism is sought to be retained in Gandhism also. The only difference in Gandhism is that the erstwhile capitalist, property-owning class will consider itself trustee on behalf of the proletariat. . . . Production will continue by unplanned private competition among the individual trustees. These conditions of production have a compelling logic of their own which lead to the same contradictions as are witnessed in capitalism today."[54] According to Hiren Mukerjee, "This apostle of pity (Gandhi) wanted a sea-change in human relationship, but he had a great deal more than the convinced conservative's caution in bringing it about: he was ready to be gentle with even flagrantly self-seeking and fundamentally anti-social vested interests; and in his preoccupation with the right kinds of means for social change, he would make compromises and concessions to the *status quo* which were often inexplicable and, in their implications, as in the idea of the rich being 'trustees' of the poor, positively pernicious."[55]

Mohit Sen reminds that in his early days Jawaharlal Nehru himself had written and spoken eloquently against the concept of trusteeship, and had even ridiculed it as being opposed to common sense and historical experiences. He writes: "It (the trusteeship idea) embodied a whole philosophy, an entire system of view with regard to the working of the whole historical process. The masses were regarded as pre-adults who had to be guided, controlled, curbed and the good life brought to them as charity from some 'messiah' on high. Not leadership, not the vanguard organization but substitution and where there was rebellion against it wholesale repression."[56]

THE ECONOMIC ORDER

The Marxist thinkers have expressed their doubts on the correctness of Sarvodaya economy with its emphasis on simple life, self-sufficiency and economic decentralization. According to Buddhadeva Bhattacharyya, "A society based on minimum exchange, small peasant production in the rural sector, minimum use of large-scale industry and maximum regional self-sufficiency can only impede the progress of technological advance and thereby human productivity. The ideal 'from each according to his capacity, to each according to his needs' is unrealizable in a society where human productivity has not registered tremendous rise. The ideal can only be realized if the reign of plenty is established which can satisfy all wants of the people. Otherwise it is a great illusion, a grand Utopia."[57]

Marxists are opposed to simple life because they differ with Gandhiji on the relationship between man and nature and on the need of limitation on the desires and wants of men. C.G. Shah says: "Since man's struggle against his environment is the fundamental fact of his existence, the interests of this struggle provide the main criterion to appraise all social institutions. How far they help this struggle is the measure of their usefulness. Thus all social institutions should be judged from this standpoint, viz., how far they are, in the final analysis, biologically valuable, how far they assist man's basic struggle against the ancient adversary, Nature."[58] He also remarks that progress in the development of productive forces is the genetic cause of all forms of progress of collective man. Technological progress is the root and condition of all other forms of human progress, social, economic, artistic, philosophical and others.[59] Hence according to him, that society can be described as progressive which, due to advance in economic production and the resultant increase of total wealth, inevitably elevates the standard of life of the toiling population and softens the element of coercion in social relations.[60] Shah considers man superior to animals because he has more desires, more wants and more needs.[61]

It is because of such ideas about social progress that Marxist thinkers are unable to reconcile themselves with Khadi as a permanent feature, with village industries, economic decentralization and other features of Sarvodaya economy. Hiren Mukerjee writes: "We hold not as a faith, but on analysis of facts, that industrialization is now, as it has always been, the one hope of the masses who everywhere in the world are still poor."[62] He also says that Gandhiji thought that a lower level of material well-being was a necessary prerequisite for a high standard of spiritual living, and that is why he came to speak of 'cottage industries', 'bread labour' and 'nature cure' as essential items on his programme for the people.[63]

An additional argument advanced by Marxists against the Sarvodaya economy has been that Gandhiji failed to revive old industries because his efforts were against the natural trend of society and the principles of economic development. Buddhadeva Bhattacharyya opines that Gandhiji's economic ideas betrayed an ignorance of the dynamism of history and failed to distinguish between industrialism and capitalism as a system, between the technological basis of modern civilization and the acquisitive institution of the private ownership of the means of production.[64] Bhattacharyya has also repeated a part of this in different words in his article on Vinoba in the context of the Sarvodaya aim of abolishing all differences between mental and manual labour. He writes: "What is the objective basis of abolition of all differences between mental and manual labour? The answer is a higher standard of living, healthier cultural life accompanied by reduction of working hours and leisure for intellectual activity."[65] And he adds later, "The correct way to put an end to the economic monopoly of big towns and cities and ensure decentralization, in its true sense, is to socialize the means of production and not to veto further increase in labour productivity.[66]

Regarding the idea of village or area self-sufficiency, Ranadive called it an 'illusion' and wrote that though "in the transition stage every endeavour should be made to protect village industries and employment, pictures of self-sufficiency are neither real nor practicable."[67]

CONCEPT OF STATE AND ITS COROLLARIES

Buddhadeva Bhattacharyya has also dealt with the Gandhian concept of state in his comprehensive study of the evolution of Gandhiji's political philosophy and with Vinoba's view on it in his recent article on him, referred to earlier. According to him, while the ultimate ideal of both Gandhiji and Vinoba was stateless society, they did not approach the problem of power from a class point of view, on which the Marxian theory of state puts its primary emphasis. To the Marxians, the state is a product of irreconcilable class antagonism, an instrument of oppression by the ruling class, and by no means an instrument of class reconciliation poised above class and parties. Gandhiji and Vinoba did not accept this view. To them, the violence of the state was not in essence violence of class domination, and hence their programme too was not of the seizure of power and they did not accept political centralization.[68] He finds the situation worse in the case of

Vinoba, since Vinoba rules out both mass action in the form of satyagraha and participation in elections to come into power.[69]

Quite similar is the criticism of Vinoba by Ranadive. He finds Vinoba's outlook on the state, organization and politics sharing many features in common with the individualistic outlook prevalent among the followers of Bakunin and Proudhon in the nineteenth century.[70]

Of Vinoba's attitude towards political parties, Bhattacharyya says: "Vinoba's description and estimate of political parties quite fits the ruling and opposition parties of the bourgeoisie in our country who profess one thing and practise the opposite. He did not recognize the vital difference between parties of the capitalist class and parties of the working class. Vinoba and his followers, because of their outlook on state and political struggle, see all evil in parties. That a political party is an indispensable weapon in the hands of exploited humanity for the ushering in of a new society is missed by them."[71] Bhattacharyya also takes objection to Vinoba's views on elections, wherein he sees them as creating new difference and breaking asunder every village and tearing it into pieces.[72] He writes, "Instead of grasping the important historical truth of Marxian criticism of bourgeois democracy, the Sarvodayites decry struggle for power as absolute evil and the rule of majority is consequently ruled out in their scheme."[73]

Besides the above objections, there is another which has been exclusively raised by Ranadive but with which others would readily concur. It pertains to decision-making by consensus which was introduced by Vinoba in Sarvodaya organization and which was strongly advocated by him for adoption in the village panchayats and other such bodies. Ranadive's objection is that it would give minority a veto over all social decisions, and thus it was liable to favour the *status quo-ists*.[74]

These are, in brief, the most important objections of Marxists against Vinoba's movement and ideas. It will be the purpose of the next chapter to examine them.

NOTES AND REFERENCES

1. *Gandhi and the CPI* in M.B. Rao (ed.), *The Mahatma: A Marxist Symposium* (People's Publishing House, 1969), p. 8.
2. ibid.
3. ibid., p. 10.
4. ibid., p. 50.
5. Gene D. Overstreet and Marshall Windmiller, *Communism in India* (University of California Press, 1959), p. 525.
6. ibid.
7. ibid., p. 526.
8. ibid. The exact words of Vinoba referred to here were: "Some are of the view that communists are destructionists. I have differed from the communists on several points and hence have criticized them at several places, but it did not appear to me that communism is destructionist in itself. It is in itself an ideology given to study and reflection. This is a great quality not found in earlier ideologies." (Hindi report of 1957 Kaladi Sarvodaya Sammelan).
9. E.M.S. Namboodiripad, *Mahatma and the Ism* (People's Publishing House, New Delhi, 1958), p. 128.
10. ibid.
11. *Sarvodaya and Communism* (Communist Party of India, 1958), pp. 6-13.
12. ibid., p. 15.
13. ibid., pp. 20-21.
14. ibid., p. 28.
15. ibid., p. 33. This criticism, as we shall also see later, has been very common and I would be dealing with it in the next Chapter. However,

the reader may be referred to the Chapter on *Sarvodaya Society — Its Political Structure* in Vishwanth Tandon's *The Social and Political Philosophy of Sarvodaya after Gandhi* (Sarva Seva Sangh Prakashan, Varanasi, 1965) and to Tandon's article on *Sarvodaya and Political Power* in *The Radical Humanist* of February 19, 1967.

16. ibid., p. 46.
17. ibid., p. 44.
18. ibid., p. 46.
19. *Gandhism After Freedom* in M.B. Rao (ed.), op. cit., p. 57.
20. ibid., pp. 62-63.
21. ibid., p. 63.
22. ibid.
23. ibid., p. 64.
24. ibid., p. 65.
25. Miraben had said in 1953: ". . . Why should the humble and the poor be told to give away part of their inadequate lands so that the right atmosphere be created for converting the rich and the proud? . . . I cannot get away from the feeling that unfair advantage is being taken of the religious and dutiful sentiments of humble villagers." She had also added: "Going on at this pace, the solution of the land problem on the Bhoodan lines would result in the landless and the semi-landless having the worst lands in the country distributed among them, while the rich would hold on to the best lands and at the same time earn credit by having their names in the lists of land donors." (Cited by Sumant Banerjee in *Vinoba and the Communist Movement* in *Gandhi Marg*, Nov-Dec. 1983 pp. 559-60). Vinoba had his own well known reasons not to agree with Miraben and then he had a vision to see that even 'the worst lands' would have great value in future, even for the purpose of agriculture.
26. Op. cit., pp. 65-66.
27. C.G. Shah, *Marxism, Gandhism, Stalinism* (Popular Prakashan, Bombay, 1963), pp. 302-303.
28. ibid., p. 303.
39. ibid., p. 307.
30. ibid.
31. ibid., p. 309.
32. ibid., p. 311. The attention of the reader may be drawn to the note in reference no. 15, and on the question of satyagraha, he may be referred to Vishwanath Tandon's article on "Vinoba and Satyagraha" in *Gandhi Marg* of October 1980. (Reprinted as Appendix in this book).

33. *Gandhi Marg*, Nov-Dec 1989, His article is captioned "Vinoba Bhave – An Ideologue of Sarvodaya: A Marxist Appraisal."
34. This is in practically all the writings of Marxists, including Namboodiripad and B. Bhattacharyya.
35. This special issue of *Gandhi Marg* is also now available as *Vinoba: The Spiritual Revolutionary* (Gandhi Peace Foundation, New Delhi, 1984, Eds. R.R. Diwakar and Mahendra Agarwal).
36. *Marxism, Gandhism, Stalinism*, pp. 244-245.
37. M.B. Rao (Ed.), op. cit., p. 26.
38. ibid., p. 56.
39. Article on Vinoba in *Gandhi Marg*, Nov-Dec., 1983.
40. *The Evolution of the Political Philosophy of Gandhi* (Calcutta Book House, Calcutta, 1969), p. 485.
41. ibid., pp. 125-126.
42. ibid., p. 128.
43. ibid., p. 501
44. ibid., p. 502.
45. C.G. Shah, op. cit., pp. 282-283.
46. *The Evolution of the Political Philosophy of Gandhi*, pp. 476-477.
47. In M.B. Rao (ed.), op. cit., p. 3.
48. E.M.S. Namboodiripad, op. cit., pp. 123-124.
49. Raghavan N. Iyer, *The Moral and Political Thought of Mahatma Gandhi* (Oxford University Press, Delhi, 1973), p. 361.
50. ibid., p. 365.
51. *Remembering Marx* (Communist Party Publication, New Delhi, 1967), p. 59.
52. *Gandhiji: A Study* (People's Publishing House, 1960), p. 211.
53. ibid., p. 213. The latest communist position on nonviolence is that "Scientific socialism does not absolutise any form of struggle, be it peaceful or violent" and that "Basing themselves on scientific socialism, Communists have always made use of the various methods of struggle available, including, of course, nonviolent methods. But Marxists have certainly a negative attitude to the Gandhian principle of *ahimsa* if it is made absolute." (*Fighters for National Liberation*, Progress Publishers, Moscow, 1983, p. 15).
54. Op. cit., p. 242. Despite the fact that in Gandhiji's own lifetime, his concept of trusteeship had been well explained by Nirmal Kumar Bose in his *Studies in Gandhism*, by M.L. Dantwala in his *Gandhism Reconsidered* and, above all, by K.G. Mashruwala in his second article on "Gandhism to Socialism" (*Harijan*, 5 December 1936),

the Marxists' misunderstanding continued. For its reasons, the reader may be referred to Vishwanath Tandon's article on "Vinoba and the Theory of Trusteeship" in the Appendix. That article was first published in an special issue of *Gandhi Marg* on Trusteeship of Nov-Dec, 1985. It contains many articles on Gandhijis theory of Trusteeship by eminent thinkers like Dada Dharmadhikari, V.K.R.V. Rao, J.D. Sethi, M.L. Dantwala and others. However, it is only Vishwanath Tandon's article which deals with the thinking of Vinoba on this issue.

55. ibid., p. 248.
56. M.B. Rao, op. cit., p. 60.
57. His article in *Gandhi Marg*, Nov.-Dec., 1983, p. 581.
58. C.G. Shah p. 53.
59. ibid., op. cit., p. 54.
60. ibid., p. 64.
61. ibid., p. 252.
62. *A Unique Leader* in M.B. Rao , op. cit., p. 75.
63. ibid, p. 76.
64. *The Evolution of the Political Philosophy of M. Gandhi*, p. 280.
65. *Gandhi Marg*, Nov-Dec., 1983, p. 581.
66. ibid., p. 582.
67. *Sarvodaya and Communism*, pp. 19-20.
68. *The Evolution of the Political Philosophy of Gandhi*, pp. 474-475.
69. His article in *Gandhi Marg,* Nov-Dec, 1983.
70. *Sarvodaya and Communism* pp. 6 and 29-30.
71. Article in *Gandhi Marg*, Nov-Dec, 1983, p. 579.
72. ibid.
73. ibid., pp. 579-80.
74. *Sarvodaya and Communism*, p. 37.

CHAPTER FOUR

Marxist Criticism Examined

The Marxist criticism of Vinoba as dealt with in the previous chapter, is divisible into two parts—one dealing with the basic premises and important Gandhian and Sarvodaya ideas[1], and the other relating to certain aspects of the post-Gandhi and post-Independence Sarvodaya movement conducted under the inspiration and guidance of Vinoba. Before examining them, however, a few observations may be made. First, as we have seen earlier, Gandhiji or Vinoba did not deny the partial truth of the Marxian social analysis, but what they urged was that the other side should also be considered and that instead of confining oneself to the externals only, one should penetrate beyond them to grasp the inner realities and be a *krantidarshi*, a seer.

Secondly, as against the close-mindedness and rigidity of Marxism, the approach of Gandhism or Sarvodaya is eclectic. Vinoba once observed: "We are universal men. We pride not on any one country, we insist not on any one religion, we do not bind ourselves to any one sect or caste. To roam about in the garden of world's best thoughts will be our diligent study, to digest them will be our constant endeavour, and to eliminate their contradictions will be our unfailing creed. To develop an attitude of universalism by synthesizing the peculiarities will be our endeavour in the realm of thought."[2] That is why he was confident that "the various one-sided ideologies, groping towards their fullness will ultimately merge in the ocean of Sarvodaya."[3] Therein also lies the explanation why Vinoba, as the Marxists themselves admitted, always tried to understand their viewpoints and Gandhiji never justified or demanded measures against the Indian communists, always looking upon them as dedicated though erring youngsters. As cited earlier, he had even said: "It is my firm conviction that nothing enduring can be built upon violence. But, be that as it may, there is no questioning the fact that the Bolshevik ideal has behind it the purest sacrifice of countless men and women who have given their all for its sake, and an ideal that is sanctioned by the sacrifices of such master spirits as Lenin cannot go in vain; the noble example of their renunciation will be emblazoned for ever and quicken and purify the ideal as time passes."[4]

Thirdly, both Marxism and Gandhism are based on different fundamental premises and world-views. Therefore there is nothing surprising in the remarks of the Marxists that the philosophy of Gandhism, characterized by religious and metaphysical prejudices and subjective illusion, is an unscientific and anti-progressive social philosophy. Buddhadeva Bhattacharyya has, in a way, admitted at several places in his *Evolution of the Philosophy of Gandhi* that his ideas are fully consistent with their basic premises. Hence it would not serve any purpose to dispute the Marxist criticism by questioning their premises, since such arguments are bound to be interminable, and the attempt being made here is to restate Gandhian ideas with necessary clarifications to remove misunderstandings and to cite in their support some modern Western thinkers who can claim to be no less rational than the Marxists claim themselves to be.

Fourthly, an important, and in a way fundamental, reason for their the vehement opposition of the Marxists to Gandhian ideas had been to differing criteria to measure the progress of society. An important test for it in Marxian thinking has been of a continuous rise in the standard of living of the common people, which does not appear to be very correct. There is much force in the reply of K.G Mashruwala to their argument that one cannot go back upon the progress which society has made in the realm of general knowledge, science, industry, art, technology and return to the past, when he says: "If one cannot consent to go back in the realm of material sciences, can one do so in the sphere of spiritual and moral development of the human race? Can we disregard the progress made by man, age after age, in the spiritual, moral, intellectual and mental spheres?"[5] A rise in the standard of living is, no doubt, beneficial to an extent, but when it goes beyond it, it adversely affects the quality of life by giving rise to consumerism. If communist countries have failed to attain their declared aim even in the economic field, one principal reason for it has been their neglect of the social and moral values based on centuries of human experiences.

NONVIOLENCE

As we have seen earlier, Marxists have been greatly opposed to the Gandhian insistence of nonviolence under all circumstances, no matter what the objective be. On the basis of Marx's oft-quoted statement that "violence is the midwife of revolution", they have been looking upon violence as somewhat inevitable for any revolutionary change. However, in this context, it would be relevant to examine the conditions in Russia where efforts for a Marxian reconstruction of society had gone on for some seventy years. There are, undoubtedly, many achievements to their credit. Immense industrial progress was made and the condition of the people was much improved but they failed to build up a new man and their ideology stands somewhat discredited.

A question which arises here is whether violence, and that too in the form of extreme coercion, was indispensable there for the above progress? Are the countries of western Europe lagging behind the USSR in this respect when they did not use the methods resorted to in Russia for the purpose? It is difficult to answer these questions in the affirmative. And then it would have to be admitted that the unexpected consequences of that violence have been undesirable. Most of the Communist Marxists are today greatly critical of the personality cult of Stalin and its consequences, though it would not be correct to lay all blame on him. According to J.D. Sethi, "Lenin and Leninism remained the Achilles' heel of both the Soviet and world communism and the source of crisis both in theory and practice of Marxism. Unless it is jettisoned in all those aspects which stifled Marxian dynamics and values, Leninism may prove to be the graveyard of world communism. Lenin succeeded in overthrowing capitalism and seizing power in a backward state but by distorting Marxism. He along with Stalin created the Soviet empire which is now collapsing."[6] However, this view of Lenin and Leninism is not acceptable to communists. An American scholar, probably of Russian origin, also differs from Sethi. He writes: "Stalinism is the sum total of perversions Stalin introduced in the theory and practice of scientific socialism. It is a phenomenon profoundly alien to Marxism and Leninism."[7] Whatever it be, one must agree with Vinoba that violence can never be the weapon of the masses and that is why the people of the USSR and other former communist countries in Europe failed to enjoy that much of freedom which they should have and the present position too is highly doubtful though the domination of the USSR over them is over. Milovan Djilas wrote in 1957: "Communist regimes are a form of latent civil war between the government and the people."[8] Thus, on the very basis of the tests of pragmatism which the Indian Communist had often urged to prove the futility of the Gandhian technique of social change the experience of the communist countries refutes them. We neither found the humanist Marx there nor any sign of withering away of the state. There are grounds to hold that they had closed their eyes to the psychological effect of the nonviolent technique on the people. It is reported that once Khruschev had expressed his surprise how India could liquidate the princely states without destroying the princes to K.P.S. Menon and then he was told that it was due to Gandhi.[9]

Hannah Arendt, it may be mentioned here, had a different interpretation of Marx's advocacy of violence, She writes: "Marx was aware of the role of violence in history, but this role to him was secondary; not violence but the contradictions inherent in the old society brought about its end. The emergence of the new society was preceded, but not caused, by violent outbreaks, which he likened to the labour pangs that precede, but of course do not cause, the event of organic brith."[10] It would also be pertinent here to point out what B.N. Ganguli has to say about Marx's attitude towards violence. According to him, when Marx stated in the *Communist Manifesto* that the history of all human societies has been the history of class struggles, he also said that it invariably ended "either in a revolutionary change, or else the common ruin of the contending classes."[11] This applies too to the conflict between the capitalist and the proletariat. It is because of the consequence of the vicious circle of violence and counter-violence that Gandhi abjured violence. Marx was also aware of the danger posed by violence, and this had led him to reject the programme of 'instant communism' in his *Critique of the Gotha Programme.*[12]

After a study of various thinkers on the issue of violence and nonviolence, Ganguli finds that violence and authoritarianism go together and that the principle of permissible violence raises a number of complex problems. The technique of combining nonviolence with it is not easy and it does not help in avoiding the vicious circle of violence and counter-violence. He also says that the ultimate change being of socio-economic character, it would be an over-simplification of reality to assume that physical force or violence is the essence of the revolutionary process.[13] However, it must be admitted that man advocated nonviolence to do so only to maintain the *status quo*. But it was neither so with Gandhiji nor Vinoba. The latter had even once observed: "If nonviolence is so defined that we have to proceed in it slowly and in a manner that it does not change society much, I am of the view that such a definition would be dangerous for nonviolence itself and very favourable to violence."[14]

PURITY OF MEANS

The principle of the purity of means emphasized in Gandhian thought, is intimately bound up with its cardinal ethical principles of Truth and Nonviolence. As far as the picture of the ideal society is concerned, there is much in common between Marxism and Sarvodaya, and this had led many to think that they differ only on the issue of the use of violence or nonviolence. But Vinoba refuted it and pointed out that there were basic differences between the two and that the difference on the use of violence is only a corollary of it.[15] However, the need of the purity of means is gradually dawning on others, Marxists or non-Marxists. Milovan Djilas wrote: "Throughout history there have been no ideal ends which were attained with non-ideal, inhuman means, just as there has been no humane society which was built by slaves. Nothing so well reveals the reality and greatness of ends as the methods used to attain them." And he further adds: "If the end must be used to condone the means then there is something in the end itself, in its reality, which is not worthy. That which really blesses the end, which justifies the efforts and sacrifices for it, is the means: their constant perfection, humaneness, increasing freedom." He also thinks that "by justifying the means because of the end, the end becomes increasingly more distant and unrealistic, while the frightful reality of the means become increasingly obvious and intolerable."[16]

Hannah Arendt also thinks that the means play a decisive role. She writes: "Since the end of human action, as distinct from the end products of fabrication, can never be reliably predicted, the means used to attain the political goals are often than not of greater relevance to the future world than the intended goals."[17] According to her, every revolutionary movement has been led by the disinterested who were motivated by compassion or by a passion for justice, and this was no less true of Marx and Lenin. However, she finds that the fury of rebellions and uprisings turned dreams into nightmares.[18] She says: "To identify the liberal national movements with such outbursts is to prophesy their doom — quite apart from the fact that the unlikely victory would not result in changing the world but only its personnel."[19] She differentiates between power and violence since power always stands in need of numbers, while violence up to a point can manage without them because it relies on implements and she writes: "Violence can always destroy power; out of a barrel of a gun grows the most effective command, resulting in the most instant and perfect obedience. What can never grow out of it is power."[20] She thinks that violence is more a weapon of reform than the revolution. It does not promote causes, but it can dramatize grievances and bring them to public attention.[21] Curiously enough, Ganguli also finds Marx observing: "An end which requires unjust means is not a just end."[22]

The changed attitude of the Indian communists towards the use of peaceful methods to attain their aims, may also be referred here though they do not subscribe to the Gandhian philosophy of nonviolence. A CPI ideologue, S.G. Sardesai said some fifteen years back: "If India is to progress as an integrated political entity, then such advance has to be brought about by nonviolent, peaceful methods. Peaceful methods are not only a virtue. They have become a historical, political necessity."[23] Sardesai does not refer here to the principle that ends do not justify means, but it is too scientific to be rejected. All the more so, when he is of the view that universal human values were recognized by Marx and Lenin.[24]

Thus, directly or indirectly, many present-day thinkers are coming closer to Gandhiji and Vinoba on the question of the purity of ends and means, though they may not yet be prepared to go to their extent. This change is both due to old and recent experiences and independent thinking on their part.

TRUSTEESHIP

The communist criticism of trusteeship principle betrays both their reluctance to see a differing viewpoint and their misunderstanding of it. Communism is rigid in its assumption that the edifice of socialism can only be built on the tomb of capitalism,. Hence they consider it to be their duty to oppose everything which they suspect to be smelling of being pro-capitalism in any way or to be a surrender to it. Consequently, they have a distorted view of Gandhiji's theory of trusteeship and the first thing needed is to clarify what it really is.

Trusteeship has two aspects, a permanent aspect and a transitional one.[25] By the first is meant that everything an individual has — be it his physical body, his intelligence or talents — has been given to him to be used for the good of society. The second aspect, the transitional one, indicates a process whereby society can be taken onwards in the direction of non-possession and non-accumulation. According to it, the first step in this direction would be to regard oneself as a trustee for one's wealth and property and finally to relinquish them altogether. The communists have missed the first aspect and failed to grasp the second in its evolutionary aspect and consequently misunderstood Gandhiji. For this, one reason is also that the word 'trusteeship' has been highly misused and has come to be equated with exploitation. The imperialists have been proclaiming themselves to be the trustee of the peoples they governed and exploited, and we are also well aware of the treatment meted out to the peoples of the 'trust' territories handed over to some of the victorious allied Powers under the Paris Settlement of 1919. That is why Vinoba has discarded that term and preferred to use the word *vishvastavritti* for it, which signifies an attitude inspiring confidence in others. Explaining it, he says: "Parents repose confidence in their children, children in their parents, and neighbours in one another. This is as it should be. Similarly there should be mutual confidence even among the various nations of the world." And he later added: "The use of one's capacities for the good of all from a feeling of confidence is implicit in individual non-possession.... We may reject the word trusteeship if we like, but we must not reject the principle of mutual confidence."[26] At another place he said: "The first implication of trusteeship is just as a father maintains and protects his son, a trustee should care more for his employees than for himself. The second is that just as a father wishes his son to become as capable as he himself is as early as possible and to stand on his own legs, in the same way a trustee should be anxious that the labour acquires ability at the earliest and becomes self-independent."[27]

Vinoba, like Gandhiji, also explained the Gandhian concept of trusteeship on several occasions. He saw in it a complete renunciation of ownership rights and stood even for the removal of a trustee if he does not use his property for public purposes. In all this, he reiterates what Gandhiji himself had made explicit at several places. Vinoba did not want a father to leave any property for his heirs.[28]

The importance of trusteeship, in its permanent aspect, is increasing in the modern world. A.E. Morgan, former chairman of the Tennessee Valley Authority in the USA has said: "Modern life with its growing complexities, greatly increases the number of situations in which the only sound relationship is that of a trustee, and the growth of a sense of responsibility has not been sufficiently rapid to meet the changing condition."[29] These days when power and authority are being centralized, it has all the more become essential for men in power or authority to use it not for their personal interests but for the good of the people. But such a feeling of trusteeship is today not sufficiently widespread and intense in either democratic or non-democratic countries. The remedy for this state of affairs lies in inculcating this feeling in all the peoples. Gandhiji had realized it and we find repeated emphasis on it in him. For the communists to denounce trusteeship in its permanent aspect amounts to belying their own process of revolution in which a predominant role has been assigned to the Party.

Coming back to the transitional aspect of trusteeship propounded by Gandhiji, communists had been wrong in thinking that it implied a perpetuation of capitalism. This is quite clear from an article of K.G. Mashruwala, published in an issue of *Harijan* in 1936 after its editing by Gandhiji. Therein Mashruwala had written: "The problem of stopping exploitation is related to, and is often held to be identical with, the institution of private property, and in Gandhi-Socialism controversies this question is perhaps discussed with greater warmth than any other. On this matter Gandhiji has perhaps more radical views than the most extreme Communist. He would like to dispossess every person of all kinds of belongings. If he tolerates the institution of private property, it is not because he loves it, or holds it necessary for the progress of humanity, but because he has yet to discover a truthful and nonviolent method of abolishing that institution."[30] Gandhiji proceeded towards it by propounding his principle of trusteeship in its transitional aspect, which with time acquired greater clarity, sharpness and a sense of urgency. This is clear from his talk with Louis Fischer in 1942 and some other statements.[31] In the trusteeship draft prepared during his detention in the Aga Khan Palace at Pune, the right to property was permitted only to the extent society permitted it for its own welfare. At one time he had even warned the rich that a violent and bloody revolution was a certainty unless there was a voluntary abdication of the riches and the power that riches gave and sharing it for the common good.[32]

As we have already seen, Vinoba's ideas on trusteeship are also very clear, and it was to help the people in the process of their relinquishment of ownership rights, that he had started the Bhoodan-Gramdan movement and asked for *sampattidan*, which meant donation of wealth, property or income. The Indian communists, as already mentioned in the earlier chapter, looked upon the Bhoodan-Gramdan movement as well-intentioned and revolutionary in concept. They were, however, critical of *sampattidan*, since they could not understand its real nature. They found fault with it because they failed to realize its full implication and saw in it a relinquishment of only a part of income accruing from wealth and property. Its aim too, like that of Gramdan, was to liberate people from the sense of ownership. It gave a start to that process by eradicating the sense of proprietorship over a part so as to bring about ultimately such a change in the individual's thinking as would lead him to a full relinquishment of his property rights. The question of wealth was much more complicated than that of land and therefore, its process of abolition could not exactly be the same. Moreover, Vinoba was of the view that if the vast rural population was liberated from its sense of ownership, it would have requisite impact on the minority population living in cities or engaged in non-agricultural callings and owning wealth and property.[33]

Several independent thinkers and scholars of the country have supported the idea of trusteeship though some are of the view that it is difficult to practise it. According to Dr V.K.R.V. Rao, "Gandhi's vision was prophetic, for the world is now aware of the inequalities that have grown in the Soviet system.

In spite of Mao's desperate attempt to destroy an emerging similar trend in China, it is pretty clear that it is only a matter of time before the inequalities of income on a large scale will re-emerge there as well. Gandhiji's doctrine of trusteeship was the only possible answer to the problem of recurring inequalities, assuming, of course, that it could be implemented in practice."[34] In this context, however, it may be pointed out that much depends upon how far the permanent principle of trusteeship has been accepted by individuals and society, and that the less need the people would feel to possess property, because of greater social security, more the idea of the relinquishment of property rights would come to be accepted. Hence for the implementation of the principle of trusteeship in society, efforts would have to be directed towards creating such social conditions which would increasingly create a sense of social security.

Though the latest position is not known, some two decades back, there was a trend in European thinking, based on experience, that neither the capitalist system nor the state capitalism of the USSR was suitable for industrial organizations and a more appropriate form would be that of trusteeship. Some experiments were also made in this direction and of them the most well known is that of Scott Bader Commonwealth.[35] One or two such experiments had also been started in India but it seems that with the decline of the Sarvodaya movement, they also suffered.[36]

ECONOMIC IDEAS

As already said in the earlier chapter, the communist thinkers were greatly opposed to the basic ideas of Gandhian economy, namely simplicity of life, economic decentralization, area or regional self-sufficiency etc. They argued that all these go against the natural trend of society and that Gandhiji failed to differentiate between industrialism and capitalism. He had no sense of the dynamism of history. But all these arguments now appear to be losing force. Many social scientists and thinkers are coming to the conclusion that the world's resources are not unlimited and the affluent living standard of the developed world would not be able to last long. However, to many a way out of it appears to lie in the development of science and technology but they too are bringing serious problems in their wake and the cultural development needed for avoiding their misuse is lagging far behind.[37] And then, the present situation as it exists is that the affluence of those countries is based on the open or hidden exploitation of the developing and undeveloped countries, and if the people of these countries try to attain the standard of living of the Western world, the unreality of the whole thing would be exposed. Hence as Gandhian economists hold, a desirable standard of living would imply fulfillment of basic necessities of men and not their greed. Gandhiji had once said, "Earth provides enough to satisfy every man's need but not for every man's greed."[38]

Some have also pointed out that consumer culture was against the very spirit of socialist economy envisaged by Marx. He did not stand for maximum consumption but for the optimum, i.e., for the satisfaction of those genuine needs which serve as a means to a richer and fuller life. He had said: "The production of many useful things result in the creation of many useless people." Besides citing the above remark of Marx, Erich Fromm says: "Marxism is humanism, and its aim is unfolding of full human potentialities. . . . Marx's concern was man, and the aim was man's liberation from the predominance of material interests, from the prison his own arrangements and deeds had built around him."[39]

In Indian conditions, economic decentralization implies a revival of village industries with the use of improved technologies. The idea of economic decentralization suited to the conditions of the countries, commands the support of such thinkers as Bertrand Russell, Erich Fromm, G.D.H. Cole and many others.[40] The new science of ecology, as indicated above, is adding a new relevance to Gandhian economic thinking. J.D. Sethi writes: "Gandhi does not need revalidation for industrial and post-industrial societies as their compulsions are pushing them into pursuing, wittingly or unwittingly, some of the Gandhian responses to the challenges facing them." And he adds: "There is a dilemma, therefore, before the world. Gandhi has already become relevant for the developed nations and one may assume that they may have to adopt a Gandhian model in the 21st century unless they find a better alternative."[41] The intellectuals, Marxists or otherwise, critical of Gandhian economy are, therefore, outdated.

In this context, it had been noteworthy that some thinkers of Eastern Europe had re-examined the issue of modern technology. For example, Mihalo Markovic of former Yugoslavia had said: "It (technology) liberates man from natural forces, but certain conditions make him a slave of his own products. It tends to eliminate his material poverty, but sometimes increases his spiritual poverty. It creates both an abundance of material goods and an overwhelming urge for property and abundance. It makes possible cultural growth of an unprecedented mass scale, but too often it provides only cheap cultural substitutes." Hence he stands "for a rational control of technological progress, for a practical annulment of its negative, inhuman consequences" and for treating it "as an important means of human liberation and fulfillment but not an end in itself."[42] Some other socialist thinkers are also critical of the runaway technology. They advocate its demystification and deworshipping.[43]

Gandhiji's and Vinoba's thinking on the issue of economy are more or less similar. They have both their local and universal elements. Whatever might have been the original, early twentieth century attitude of Gandhiji expressed in *Hind Swaraj* on machinery, his subsequent clarifications give ample proof of his rational thinking on the issue. J.D. Sethi observes: "The supreme difficulty facing a serious analyst of Gandhi is that almost every statement about him is little more than a half-truth and the trouble with half-truths is the other half. There is an additional difficulty; every statement made by Gandhi himself is also a partial truth, made deliberately so as to take a new step towards some larger truth. The half-truths distort Gandhi and Gandhi's partial truths demand a massive intellectual effort to comprehend him."[44]

Vinoba developed Gandhiji's ideas further in the light of the changed conditions of the country and the world and of the unprecedented advance in science, differentiating it from technology. His attitude had been: "I am not an irrationalist. I shall have machines considered necessary."[45] He had divided machines in the three categories of time-saving, productive and destructive. While he was unreservedly opposed to destructive machines, his attitude towards the other two was pragmatic.[46]

Neither Gandhiji nor Vinoba favoured pauperism. It is not what is meant when they advocate 'simplicity'. It is 'voluntary simplicity' and therefore something different. They simply did not confuse a high standard of living with a high standard of life, but they knew that for a high standard of life, a basic minimum of living was a must. Gandhiji's anxiety to remove the poverty of the Indian masses to whom God could only appear in the form of food, is well-known. The same had been with Vinoba, who many a time referred to an incident in the life of Lord Buddha, who advised his disciple to give food to a hungry man first before preaching his message to him.

The communists and many other intellectuals failed to understand other Gandhian economic ideas as well. Gandhiji's concept of self-sufficiency is intimately linked with that of the Swadeshi which had no narrowness in it. Gandhiji had once observed: "To reject foreign manufactures merely because they are foreign, and to go on wasting national time and energy to the promotion in one's own country of manufactures for which it is not suited would be criminal folly, and a negation of Swadeshi spirit."[47] And according to Vinoba, "The idea of self-sufficiency is often misunderstood. It is certainly not opposed to wider cooperation. It need not be an isolating factor. I wish that people cooperate consciously (intentionally) on as wide a scale as possible. From the village republic to the world government there can be a continuous and widening sphere of intelligent cooperation in which all will help each other."[48] Self-sufficiency in the basic and primary needs of life increases the ability of the people to resist tyranny or domination, domestic or foreign.

The concept of decentralization too had been mistaken for "going back to the antiquated mode of production", which it is not. Vinoba's attitude towards industries was not negative but pragmatic. He was for liberating man from unnecessary labour so as to free energy for higher pursuits. Keeping that aim in mind he had expressed his dissent from a title of Gandhiji's collection, "*Industrialize and Perish*", and had said that: "When we affirm that decentralization will disintegrate the machine age, what I mean to convey is that we shall disintegrate it after we have drawn out all that is good in it. The former non-centralized village industries lacked this power of digesting and assimilating the advantage of the machine age. This is the fundamental difference between purposeful decentralized industries and the old non-centralized village industries."[49] And on another occasion, he had said: "What is to be understood is that though in the beginning the new technology has resulted in the exploitation of man, yet I hold that it has a purpose to serve in the world, which is to liberate man from unnecessary labour he has been compelled to do so far. It is possible to achieve it if proper use is made of technology. Hence I have faith that the prevailing idea of industrialism will lose its hold after it has done good. I do not consider it to be a curse. It has many demerits but the next step would only follow when its good points have been assimilated."[50]

THE CONCEPT OF STATE AND POLITICAL DECENTRALIZATION

A communist looks upon the state as a class institution, a conspiracy of the rich and powerful to exploit the weak, the have-nots. Hence they aim at a classless and stateless society. But their road to it passes through the intensification of state called "the dictatorship of the proletariat." To Gandhiji the state, as mentioned in an earlier chapter, represents violence in a concentrated and organized form and was a soulless machine which could never be weaned away from violence. According to Avijit Pathak, "As a matter of fact, beneath Gandhi's fear of the modern state lay his firm conviction that it would ultimately lead to the creation of a new power elite."[51] And if so this fear of his was not baseless as shown by the Soviet Union's experience. Mohit Sen, a CPI member, acknowledged it in his article on assessing "Stalin and Stalinism" when he wrote: "The growth of the bureaucracy and the bureaucratic mentality had its inevitable concomitant corruption, the growth of hierarchy and vested interests and infringement on social power, justice and values."[52] Hence the path that Gandhiji had chosen for the development of his stateless society was primarily of both developing appropriate character in the people and restructuring society in a manner helpful to the development of that character. Further as J.D. Sethi observes: "The Gandhian process of social change and transformation depends upon the creation of a revolutionary elite minority which will be the elite class in the best sense of the term. This class will have to identify itself with the masses by denying itself most of the material advantages, probably in proportion to the power it exercises. The self-conscious moral revolutionary minority will set ethical standards and principles first for its own practice and then society for its restructuring."[53] This reliance on an elite for the restructuring of a new society resembles the Leninist process only in principles but not in practice. It is so because it thought of imposition from above and not of the conversion of the people by both examples and precepts. Avijit Pathak has also rightly said: "Gandhi wanted people to choose their own affairs, to decide their own fate with the help of their cultural idioms."[54]

Vinoba understood Gandhiji much better than many who claim to know him and if his ideas and programmes are analysed, one finds that he followed the path Gandhiji had chalked out for the reconstruction of Indian society with some necessary changes, demanded by the altered conditions of post-war and post-Independence India. There is evidence to show that his attitude towards political power and political parties, for which both Ranadive and Buddhadeva Bhattacharyya have criticized him, is similar to that of Gandhiji. Movement for independence apart, Gandhiji relied on his constructive programmes and satyagraha for the creation of his new society. He never participated in an election meeting and never exercised his franchise though it is highly doubtful if he had a vote at all. It was even said that if any constructive worker desired to participate in satyagraha, he was advised to resign first from the constructive organization.[55] His advice to a body of constructive workers in December 1947 was to keep out of politics altogether. He had said to them: "The objective of the constructive work organization is to generate political power. But if we may say that political power having come, it must be ours as a prize for our labours, it would degrade us and spell our ruin." He had also told then that in Sevagram he had depreciated the proposal of his people to enroll as voters, and he had further said: " Today, politics has become corrupt. Anybody who goes into politics is contaminated. Let us keep out of it altogether. Our influence will grow thereby. The greater our inner purity, the greater will be our hold on the people, without any effort on our part."[56] And he did not content himself with only this. He even advised the Congress in his "The Last Will and Testament" to disband its organizations and to flower into a Lok Sevak Sangh.[57] Such was the thinking and practice of Gandhiji with which Vinoba agreed.

It should also be emphasized here that Vinoba was basically a constructive worker with a constructive bent of mind, seeking the cooperation of all, peoples and parties, for his movement aiming at a social revolution. Any participation in politics would have worked against it. There is reason to hold that the huge response Vinoba appeared to have received at the Gaya Sarvodaya Sammelan in 1954, had alarmed the Congress leaders who ultimately adopted an indifferent attitude towards the Bhoodan movement while maintaining outward cooperation. It may also be mentioned here that a prominent RSS leader, Nanaji Deshmukh, who had also been a cabinet minister in Morarji Desai's Government, gave up politics altogether in 1980 on finding that it went ill with his constructive activities undertaken under the Deendayal Upadhyaya Trust, to which he accorded primacy.

Another reason for Vinoba refusing to involve himself in politics and to accord the Sarvodaya workers the same advice, was his belief that no revolutionary thought could be propagated through the power of the state. He said once: "The decline of the Buddhist faith in India dates from the date (day) it received the backing of the government power. When the Christian faith was backed by the imperial power of Constantine, it became Christian only in name."[58] To Acharya Kripalani who had argued that without taking power in one's hands, it was not possible to establish the social order of Gandhian conception, his reply was: "Is not the power in our hands today? If we hold that by taking (away) the power from those who are wielding it today, we shall be able to do better, we are very much mistaken."[59] On another occasion, he had said: "People often ask me why I am out of politics and why I do not accept responsibility in the government of the nation, I answer, 'Two bullocks have already been yoked to the cart; of what use it would be to take me as a third? The best way (path) for me is to repair the road so that it can travel in the right direction."[60]

However, it did not mean that he attached no importance

to politics. He once said: "We do not deny the importance of politics, nor do we want to run away from it. This is not escapism. On the other hand, our policy is based on stark realism. We want to change the spirit of politics."[61] What he was referring here to was his efforts to replace *rajniti*, the politics of the state, by *lokniti*, the politics of the people, in which the people would not be mere spectators but active participants. And then, his attitude towards the state was not as unfavourable as was generally held. Though he differentiated between nonviolence and penal power of the state, he would not class the latter as 'violence'. He regarded the emergence of the state as a form of social organization, an improvement over the earlier condition of violent anarchy and as marking a step in the evolution of society from the condition of violence to that of nonviolence. He, of course, regarded it to be an intermediary stage and held that the social fulfilment lay in rising to the higher stage when man would need no coercive authority to regulate his conduet.[62]

The realist Vinoba looked upon all such legislations as nonviolent which commanded the moral support of the people. He had even demanded prohibition of cow slaughter by law. However, he considered his main role to lie in preparing the mind of the people for it.[63] When Vinoba talked of *lokniti*, the politics of the people, he thought in terms of political decentralization like Gandhiji. It was quite natural for the communists to oppose it since they have been standing for the dictatorship of the party, which they preferred to identify with the proletariat. As against political decentralization, they stood for 'democratic centralism'. But several eminent western thinkers have lent their support to the idea of decentralization in one way or another, though they do not go to the extent of Gandhiji or Vinoba since their tradition, their problems and the alternatives before them had been different. They do so because they were perturbed at the growing 'alienation' and 'dehumanization' in their society and at the formal or the inorganic nature of their democracies. To remove these defects, they had been compelled to think in terms of devolution or decentralization. These are, no doubt, two different things, especially in their spirit, but in early stages decentralization can have its beginning only in devolution in any centralized government. While Bertrand Russell pleads for devolution laying down the general principle that smaller bodies should be left with those functions which do not prevent the larger bodies from fulfilling theirs.[64] Erich Fromm talked of decentralization. He has been of the view that so far the development of democracy has been in the extension of franchise but its further progress lay in recognizing that true democracy cannot be attained in an atmosphere of mass voting but only in relatively small group corresponding to the old Town Meetings, where the issues can be discussed thoroughly and people have personal contact with each other which makes it more difficult for demagogic and irrational influences to work on their minds.[65] He also says elsewhere: "The aim of humanistic socialism can be attained only by the introduction of maximum decentralization compatible with a minimum of centralization necessary for the functioning of an industrial society. . . . The functions of a centralized state must be reduced to a minimum, while the voluntary activity of freely cooperating citizens constitute the control mechanism of social life."[66] However, it is G.D.H. Cole who approaches Sarvodaya most when he writes: "I am neither a Communist nor a Social Democrat, because I regard both as a creed of centralization and bureaucracy, whereas I feel sure that a socialist society that is true to its equalitarian principle of human brotherhood must rest on the widest possible diffusion of power and responsibility so as to enlist the participation of as many as possible of its citizens to the task of democratic self-government."[67] He is also cited to have said: "The decay of parliaments has accompanied the democratization of electorate not because democracy is wrong, but because we have allowed the growth of huge political organizations to be accompanied by the atrophy of smaller ones, on which alone they can be securely built.[68] Thus there is a quest for community and Robert A. Nisbet says: " The liberal values of autonomy and freedom of personal choice are indispensable to a genuinely free society, but we shall achieve and maintain these only by resting them in the conditions in which liberal democracy will thrive — diversity of culture, plurality of association, and division of authority."[69]

All this thinking is post-war thinking with the experience of the Soviet Union before them and it goes against the communist criticism of Gandhian political decentralization. However, one must admit that the present experience with the Panchayats and other local bodies has been unfortunate. But its causes lie elsewhere and not in the Gandhian conception being wrong. It is primarily due to the importation of party politics in them and in the general degradation of public life observed in the present-day India. Vinoba had an inkling of it and he wanted the Panchayats to be kept free of political parties and go to work on the principle of consensus which too had been looked upon with disfavour by the communists.[70] It would be considered later under the next section.

OBJECTIONS TO VINOBA'S MOVEMENT

As regards the Marxist objection to the technique adopted in the Sarvodaya movement inspired and led by Vinoba mentioned in the earlier chapter, one must admit that it is certainly difficult to defend some aspects of it. For example, requisite precautions were not observed for the correctness of the statistics of the lands donated in Bhoodan and it is also true that a good part of the land was found unfit for distribution for one reason or another. But all this was quite natural. The inexperience and over-enthusiasm of the workers was responsible for the first mistake, while the second is not surprising in a movement of such dimension as Bhoodan was. Moreover, Vinoba had the foresight to realize the value and importance of every bit of land, even if unarable, in future India, and so he did not mind it.

There can also be no denying the fact that of the target of fifty million acres laid down by Vinoba for obtaining under Bhoodan, not even ten per cent was realized. Vinoba was aware of its impossibility but he had fixed such a high target because of the nature of Indians who are only inspired to work if the target is high.[71] And, then, the communists themselves, as mentioned in the earlier chapter, had been of the view that the objective of the movement was desirable and the workers were sincere in their efforts. Moreover, it is beyond dispute that the land distributed under the movement was more than the land distributed by the State governments which had been motivated to do so by the Bhoodan movement itself, when formerly even their best legislation abolishing the Zamindari system had altogether ignored the claims of the agricultural landless labourers even to the lands they were actually cultivating.[72] Thus a great achievement of the Bhoodan-Gramdan movement* was to highlight their claim and to arouse

* The movement which has its beginning as Bhoodan movement in 1951 had in 1955 become converted into Bhoodan-Gramdan movement with special emphasis on Gramdan.

sympathy for them. Another big achievement of the Bhoodan-Gramdan movement was that it attacked the very concept of private property, which the communists, in spite of it being in accord with their thinking, had not been able to do. None also can refuse to give to Vinoba the credit for showing a way to build up the power of the people and to infuse in them some faith in themselves. If the movement is 'dead' now, its causes lie primarily elsewhere than in the mistakes attributed to it.

The criticism of the movement for *sampattidan* on the ground of neglect of the state power, has already been dealt with earlier and it needs no repetition. But it is different with the charge that Vinoba gave up the Gandhian method of nonviolent resistance in his movement, doing harm to the struggle of toiling people. This criticism is shared by even many non-Marxists, Dr Rammanohar Lohia being the most prominent of them. The Western pacifists too were critical of Vinoba for it and they influenced some important Sarvodaya workers as well. Hence it needs examination.

Undoubtedly, Vinoba's general attitude towards the method of nonviolent resistance used by Gandhiji in the freedom struggle and looked upon as his great contribution throughout the world, had not been favourable, though he had permitted it on certain issues and himself had gone on fast on two occasions. The main reasons for his attitude were three.[73]

First, he was keen to develop another aspect of satyagraha which was implied in it and had been left undeveloped during the freedom struggle, though Gandhiji can be said to have experimented with it in 1947 in Noakhali. It aimed at what was termed 'non-violent assistance in right thinking', which was expected to bring about a change of heart as well. Vinoba felt that in democratic India, there was not much place for a method used for freeing the country. We cannot demand from our countrymen to quit the country as we could with foreigners and what was presently required was a satyagraha which is more effective in changing the mind and heart. Hence he thought of gentle and gentler small satyagraha. None can deny the force of his argument, though one may feel that nonviolent resistance has not fully outlived its utility. Vinoba recognized it and permitted it provided some conditions were fulfilled. Laying them down, he once said: "If a democratic government does grave injustice and the hearts of the persons at the helm do not melt while righteous men feel that a grave injustice is being done, satyagraha (nonviolent resistance) may become necessary and I say that no one can rule out such satyagraha."[74]

Secondly, that important weapon was being greatly misused after independence. The communists had even started the process earlier and Gandhi had reprimanded them for it in his own way, but now it was becoming general. So much so that even a scholar interested in Gandhiji had to observe: "A review of the contemporary history of political events in India suggests that *duragraha* and demonstrations, strike and fasting — under the name of satyagraha — are the techniques of the day."[75] It seemed to justify the fears of many who had warned Gandhiji that it might breed in the people a spirit and habit of indiscipline and anarchy. Thirdly, Vinoba also feared that with enemy countries around us, it was liable to weaken the country and hence should be avoided.[76]

So much about Vinoba and satyagraha, and now the only criticism which remains to be examined is one made by Ranadive that Vinoba's plea for decisions at various level on the principle of consensus, provided a veto to the minority and was unsuited to build a new social order. There are two words in Hindi *sarvasammati* and *sarvanumati*. The English equivalent of the former is 'unanimity' while the latter means 'permission of all' and is translated as 'consensus'. While the first implies full agreement of all, some disagreement is possible in the latter if it is not to the extent of outright rejection and others are permitted to have their way. On Vinoba's advice, the principle of consensus had been adopted as a rule in Sarvodaya institutions but it had merely remained as a plea for Panchayats and other higher institutions. When differences had cropped up in the 1970s in the Sarvodaya organization itself between Vinoba and Jayaprakash Narayan on the issue of support to the students movement in Bihar and the movement for 'Total Revolution', many on the side of Jayaprakash Narayan had been irked by it, but Vinoba had remained steadfast in its support to the principle.

It was natural for Ranadive to object to it because the whole thinking of communism is based on conflict and lack of faith in others. It is otherwise with the Gandhian thinking though it admits in society the existence of conflict. Its attempt is to make society rise above it and it does not believe that its process lies in intensifying them as communism does. Vinoba had once said: "All the efforts made by men in the world are aimed at becoming one in love. Some conflicts, and some disputes too, appear to be there, and some have built up an elaborate philosophy of struggle, but these conflicts and struggles do not last long. They come and go, but man's life, full of love, goes on."[77] And he also said: "I want revolution but I also want peace. Without peace, India cannot survive. And without revolution, the poor in India would know no end to their misery. If we adhere to aggressive or violent methods, we are bound to seek shelter, like Pakistan, of some expert military Guru. Hence I insist on peaceful and nonviolent revolution."[78]

In going in for consensus, Vinoba has been influenced by the working on its principle by the village Panchayats in ancient and medieval India and by the practice of the Quakers. As against it, Ranadive borrowed the system of decision-making by majority which he supported, from the working of Western democracies. But that system too had come for criticism from some eminent western political scientists and thinkers. One of them is Prof. E. Barker. He finds that the sole justification of decision by majority is that its will can be made to prevail in society, something which goes against the very concept of democracy. He argues that a democracy should be able to enlist and elicit, as far as is humanly possible, the thought, the will and the general capacity of everyone of its members.[79] He also says: "It must be a government depending upon the mutual interchange of ideas, a mutual criticism of the ideas interchanged, and on the common and agreed choice of the idea which emerges triumphant from the ordeal of interchange and criticism."[80]

Erich Fromm has also criticized the system of majority vote. He writes that in our age of conformity, the democratic method has more and more assumed the meaning that a majority decision is necessarily right, and morally superior to that of the minority. This is obviously an error; in fact, all 'right' ideas were originally the ideas of minorities.[81]

Thus, if consensus has some drawbacks, the majority system strikes at the very roots of democracy all the more so, since in the present age all kinds of minorities are getting conscious of their rights and are prepared to fight for them. Experience shows that the habit of decisions by consensus can be developed in society[82] and it has the possibility of reforming the individuals and society of its unsocial tendencies, while, on the other hand, the majority system would only further strengthen them. However, the change would have to be brought about gradually, beginning in the Indian context with the Panchayats, Panchayat Samities and Zila Parishads as once suggested by Shriman Naryan in a speech in Hyderabad. He had also rightly said then that it was rather necessary for their success also and would need intensive education and training for the rural masses and some incentive to those bodies too in the form of material and financial concessions to work in a spirit of harmony and unity.[83]

It is, however, a different mater that in the present state of social and political degradation in India both the systems can be manipulated because of the nexus between the politicians, the criminals, the rich and the bureaucracy. But a way has to be found to remedy this state of affairs and it has been correctly said: "There is only one force which can reform the world. That force is faith in man. . . . It is the only realism that we can afford, for anything else will lead to rapid destruction."[84] And it may be hoped that in the present crisis and the state of despair, we may realize the dire need of it. Herein lies the value and superiority of the Gandhian thought. Gandhiji had said in 1920: " I refuse to suspect human nature. It will, is bound to respond to any noble and friendly action."[85] And again in 1942: "In the application of the method of nonviolence, one must believe in the possibility of every person, however depraved, being reformed under humane and skilled treatment."[86] The same has been the thinking of Vinoba who said in 1953: "A man's heart, we must understand, is always good at the core. It may get rusted outside due to various external factors, but its internal goodness always remains the same, whatever the outward appearance. It is, as I often say, like a cabbage whose outer layer may go bad but the layers inside retain their freshness."[87]

NOTES AND REFERENCES

1. I am inclined to take Gandhism and Sarvodaya as synonymous. The monthly organ of the Gandhi Seva Sangh was titled *Sarvodaya* and the Hindi version of Gopinath Dhawan's *The Political Philosophy of Mahatma Gandhi* is titled *Sarvodaya Tattva-Darshan*. Hence I look upon Gandhi as the father of the Sarvodaya school of thought.
2. Vinoba, *Samanvaya* (Sarva Seva Sangh Prakashan, Varanasi, 1965), p. 3.
3. Introduction to Jayaprakash Narayan, *From Socialism to Sarvodaya* (SSS Prakashan, Varanasi, 1959).
4. *Young India*, November 15, 1928.
5. K.G. Mashruwala, *Gandhi and Marx* (Navajivan Publishing House, Ahmedabad, 1951), pp. 60-61.
6. J.D. Sethi, *Lenin Sitting on the Throat of Marx* in *Mainstream* of April 28, 1990, p. 15.
7. Cited in Mohit Sen, *Assessing Stalinism and Communism*, in *Mainstream* of June 23, 1990, p.12.
8. *The New Class* (Frederick A. Praegar, New York, 1957), p. 87.
9. According to K.P.S. Menon who was then the Indian Ambassador in Soviet Union, Khruschev had exclaimed to him, "You Indians are an amazing people! How on earth did you manage to liquidate Princely rule without liquidating the Princes?" Menon replied, "Because of Mahatma Gandhi." (*Indian Express* of September 12, 1976).
10. *On Violence* (Allen Lane, The Penguin Press, London, 1970), p. 11.
11. B.N. Ganguli, *Gandhi's Social Philosophy* (Vikas Publishing House, New Delhi, 1973), pp. 360 and 362. (Second edition published in 2000 by National Gandhi Museum).
12. ibid., p. 362.
13. ibid., pp. 9, 411 and 419.
14. Kusum Deshpande, *Kranti Ki Oar* (SSS Prakashan, Varanasi, 1956), p. 127.
15. Vinoba's Introduction to Mashruwala, *Gandhi and Marx*, pp. 8-15.
16. *The New Class*, pp. 162-63.
17. *On Violence*, p. 4.
18. ibid., pp. 24 and 21.
19. ibid., p. 21.
20. ibid., pp. 42 and 53.
21. ibid., p. 79.
22. B.N. Ganguli, *Gandhi's Social Philosophy*, p. 396 (Second edition published in 2000 by National Gandhi Museum).

23. S.G. Sardesai, *Gorbachev and India Today* in *Mainstream* of April 29, 1989, p. 22.
24. ibid., p. 24.
25. Dada Dharmadhikari, *Sarvodaya Darshan* (SSS Prakashan, Varanasi, 1958), p. 287.
26. Introduction to Mashruwala, *Gandhi and Marx,* pp. 25 and 26.
27. Nirmala Deshpande, *Kranti Ki Rah Par* (SSS Prakashan, Varanasi, 1958), p. 112.
28. Vishwanath Tandon, *Selections from Vinoba* (SSS Prakashan, Varanasi, 1981), pp. 73-75.
29. *The Long Road* (Navajivan, Ahmedabad, 1950), p. 75.
30. This article has been reproduced in Mashruwala, *Gandhi and Marx* from the *Harijan* of December 5, 1936 on pp. 98-101.
    Besides Mashruwala, there are a number of articles which explain and support the Gandhian principle of trusteeship. Nirmal Kumar Bose's article in his *Studies of Gandhism* (Calcutta, 1948) was written before Gandhiji's death. For recent thinking, one may refer to the *Gandhi Marg* of Nov.-Dec., 1985 which exclusively deals with trusteeship. It contains articles by Dr. J.D. Sethi, Dr V.K.R.V. Rao, Ravindra Varma and some others. One by Vishwanath Tandon is on *Vinoba and the Theory of Trusteeship.* That article is being reproduced here as an appendix.
31. Louis Fischer, *A Week with Gandhi* (International Book House, Bombay, 1944), p. 43. Also Tendulkar, Vol. VI, p. 98.
32. M.K. Gandhi, *Trusteeship* (Ahmedabad, 1960), pp. 39-40.
33. The reader may be here referred to Vishwanath Tandon's article on *Bhoodan Gramdan* in the *Gandhi Marg*, Nov-Dec, 1983 issue.
34. *The Gandhian Alternative to Western Socialism* (Bharatiya Vidya Bhavan, Bombay, 1970), p. 51.
35. Folkert, Wilken, *New Forms of Ownership in Industry* (SSS Prakashan, Varanasi, 1962). E.F. Schumacher, *Small Is Beautiful* (Radha Krishna, New Delhi, 1977) also gives a good account of Scott Bader Commonwealth on pp. 256-64.
36. K. Arunachalam, *Applied Trusteeship* in *Gandhi Marg*, Nov-Dec, 1985.
37. There is a lot of literature pertaining to the problem of limited resources and ecological danger. Schumacher writes: "An attitude to life which seeks fulfilment in the single-minded pursuit of wealth – in short, materialism does not fit into this world, because it contains within itself no limiting principle, while the environment in which it is placed is strictly limited. Already, the environment is trying to tell

us that certain stresses are becoming excessive. As one problem is being 'solved', ten new problems arise as a result of the first 'solution'. As Professor Barry Commoner emphasizes, the new problems are not the consequences of incidental failure but of technological success." *Small is Beautiful*, p. 25.

38. Cited in Pyarelal, *Towards New Horizon* (Navajivan, Ahmedabad, 1959), p. 12.
39. Erich Fromm (ed.), *Socialist Humanism: An International Symposium* (Allen Lane, The Penguin Press, London, 1967), pp. 215 and 208.
40. The prominent thinkers supporting the idea of economic decentralization include Bertrand Russell (*Authority and the Individual*), Erich Fromm (*The Sane Society*), G.D.H. Cole (*A History of Socialist Thought*, Vol. V) and E.F. Schumacher (*Small Is Beautiful*). The last book is wholly a plea for decentralization.
41. *Gandhian Values and 20th Century Challenges* (Govt. of India, Publications Division, New Delhi, 1979), pp. 27 and 28.
42. Erich Fromm, *Socialist Humanism*, p. 87.
43. ibid., pp. 318-19.
44. J.D. Sethi, op. cit., p. 3.
45. *Krant Darshan,* Varanasi, 1962, p. 133.
46. Vishwanath Tandon, *Selections from Vinoba* (Varanasi, 1981), p. 144.
47. *Yeravda Mandir* (Ahmedabad, 1945), p. 66.
48. *Bhoodan*, August 22, 1956.
49. Introduction to Mashruwala, *Gandhi and Marx*, p. 27.
50. Vishwanath Tandon, *Selections from Vinoba*, p. 143.
51. *Mainstream* of October 7, 1989, p. 17.

    In this context, it is interesting to point out what Rajni Kothari has to say. According to him, "Gandhi's advocacy of decentralization of both economic and political power was based on a shrewd realization of the dangerous consequences of the Westminister model of politics when transplanted from a small and progressive society to a large and extremely poor society ridden by great divisions and inequality. Gandhi's successors forgot all about his insight and gradually paved the way for a centralized state in which manipulation rather than participation became the rule." *Democratic Polity and Social Change in India: Crisis and Opportunities*, Allied Publishers, New Delhi, 1976, p. 128.
52. Mohit Sen, *Assessing Stalin and Stalinism* in *Mainstream*, 1989 Annual Issue, p. 137.

53. J.D. Sethi, *Gandhian Values and 20th Century Challenges,* p. 46.
54. *Mainstream*, October 7, 1989, p. 17.
55. Vinoba in *Harijan*, September 1, 1951, p. 229.
56. D.G. Tendulkar, *Mahatma*, Vol. VIII, p. 234.
57. Pyarelal, *Towards New Horizon* (Navajivan, Ahmedabad, 1959), Appendix B.
58. Vinoba, *Democratic Values* (SSS Prakashan, Varanasi, 1962), p. 18.
59. *Harijan*, June 19, 1949, p. 126.
60. Vinoba, *Third Power* (Varanasi, 1972), p. 21.
61. *Bhoodan*, December 12, 1956, p.3.
62. Vinoba, *Third Power*, pp. 21-22. Vinoba, *From Bhoodan to Gramdan* (Sarvodaya Prachuralaya, Tanjore, 1957)), p. 22. Vinoba, *Lokniti* (Varanasi 1959), p. 167.
63. *Bhoodan*, April 17, 1957, p.1 and *Third Power,* pp. 20-21.
64. Bertrand Russell, *Authority and the Individual* (Allen and Unwin, London, 1955), pp. 98-100.
65. Erich Fromm, *The Sane Society* (Routledge, London, 1956), p. 340.
66. Eric Fromm, "The Basis of Humanistic Socialism" in *Bhoodan*, March 22, 1960.
67. G.D.H. Cole, *A History of Socialist Thought,* Vol. V (London, 1960), p. 337.
68. Cited in Robert A. Nisbet, *The Quest for Community* (Oxford University Press, 1977), p. 255.
69. Robert A. Nisbet, op. cit., p. 279.
    However, according to Arthur E. Morgan, "The small community of the future will be neither a replica of the village of the past, nor a surrender to the city. It will be a new creation, uniting the values of both, and largely avoiding their limitations." (*The Community of the Future and the Future of Community,* Hindustani Talimi Sangh, Wardha, 1958, p. 55).
70. Vinoba, *Democratic Values*, p. 119.
    For his opinion on political parties, one may be referred to relevant passages in Vishwanath Tandon (ed.), *Selections from Vinoba* (National Gandhi Museum, New Delhi, 2004).
71. As 1957 approached, Vinoba was repeatedly questioned on the attainment of the target of fifty million acres of land and this statement is based on his various replies.
72. The UP Act abolishing the Zamindari system had been considered to be the best in the whole country but the claims of the landless

agricultural labourers to the lands getting vested in the Gram Sabhas had been fully overlooked. He was not entitled to it at all.

T.K. Ommen who is quite critical of some aspects of the Bhoodan movement, observed: "Notwithstanding the scathing criticisms levelled against the Bhoodan movement from several quarters, on the whole its achievements are substantial. Although the collection and distribution of land through the movement fall short of the targets fixed by the Bhoodan leaders, even in this respect the achievements are considerable compared with the state efforts in securing surplus land for distribution to the landless through the imposition of ceiling laws." *25 Years of Bhoodan Gramdan* in *Everyman's Weekly* of June 15, 1975. The land distributed under Bhoodan was 12,85,738 acres (*Savodaya*, July-Aug 1975), while by the end of 1982, the government distribution was 10,88,000 acres (*The Times of India*, April 2, 1983).

73. Vinoba's attitude towards nonviolent resistance has been discussed more fully in Vishwanath Tandon's article on *Vinoba and Satyagraha*, reproduced here as an appendix.
74. *Harijan*, February 20, 1952.
75. Joan V. Bondurant, *Conquest of Violence* (Oxford University Press, 1959), p. 44.
76. Vinoba had expressed this view particularly in the context of the Bihar Movement.
77. *Bhoodan-Yajna*, November 4, 1955.
78. *Harijan*, August 14, 1954.
79. E. Barker, *Reflections on Government* (London, 1948), pp. 35-36.
80. ibid., p. 36.
81. Erich Fromm, *The Sane Society* (Routledge, London, 1956), p. 330. For a detailed discussion of Vinoba's views on consensus, see Vishwanath Tandon, *The Social and Political Philosophy of Sarvodaya after Gandhi* (Varanasi, 1965), pp. 126-32.
82. An example of it can be seen in Arthur E. Morgan, *The Community of the Future and the Future of Community* (Hindustani Talimi Sangh, Wardha, 1958), pp. 97-98.
83. *Indian Express,* July 22, 1961.
84. *Manas*, Februrary 6, 1958. *Manas* was a periodical published in the U.S.A.
85. N.K. Bose, *Selections from Gandhi* (Navajivan, Ahmedabad, 1948), p. 28.
86. ibid.
87. *Harijan*, December 19, 1953.

CHAPTER FIVE

Which Way Lies Hope?

The heading of this chapter has been borrowed from the title of a book of Richard B. Gregg, published in its revised edition in 1957. It examines both capitalism and communism and finds them wanting from the philosophical, social and economic points of view, and upholds the Gandhian thinking in general and its economic programme for India in particular. The book takes into account a few ecological problems as well, such as soil erosion, decreased water supply, squandering of natural resources, increase in world population and a few others. However, by that time, the ecological problems had not acquired the dimension they did in the sixties when Carson's *The Silent Spring* rang the bell of alarm about pollution which as time passes is causing more and more worry for the survival of humanity.

By the end of that decade, the problem had become so serious that the Secretary General had to submit a report on it to the United Nations in May 1969. He said: "For the first time in the history of mankind, there is arising a crisis of worldwide proportions involving developed and developing countries alike — the crisis of human environment. Portents of the crisis have long been apparent — in the explosive growth of human populations, in the poor integration of a powerful and efficient technology with environmental requirements, in the deterioration of agricultural lands, in the unplanned extension of urban areas, in the decrease of available space and the growing danger of extinction of many forms of animal and plant life. It is becoming apparent that if current trends continue, the future of life on earth could be endangered."[1]

He even found fault with the construction of large dams, water reservoirs and canals. When constructing them, while the economic and engineering factors are given full weight, broader environmental impact is inadequately considered. The report, however, expressed its greatest worry on the question of pollution of all kinds, including that by solid waste. It said: "The greatest apparent man-made changes in the biological environments are those related to pollution. These include the increase of carbon dioxide, particulate matter, and various toxic and radioactive materials in the atmosphere which could have long-term deleterious effects and must be studied and where necessary controlled."[2] It, while admitting the need of industrialism to raise the living standards of the people, also pointed out that the side effects of poorly planned or uncontrolled industrialization and of the one-sided application of technology have been a direct cause of many serious environmental problems.[3]

As a result of it combined with the publication of the *Limits to Growth*, the statement of the 33 eminent British scientists in 1972 and the Stockholm Conference on Environment (1972), the world became conscious of the possibility of environmental disaster. Many books were published in the seventies on the subject and they included Arnold J. Toynbee's *Surviving the Future* (1971) and *Mankind and Mother Earth* (1976). However, the thinking and enthusiasm generated for an ecological way of life subsided greatly later on due to the lure of a higher and higher standard of living. Marxism with its belief in such a standard is incapable of raising its voice against it, though the life of Marx himself and of the communist workers in general belie it. It is different with Gandhian thought. A cardinal principle of Gandhian economy is simplicity of life since it holds that there is enough in the world to satisfy its needs but not its greed. To Gandhiji, a test of any civilized society or individual was restriction on wants and not their multiplication.

The dangers facing the world are both internal and external. The environmental problem is an external danger while the internal danger lies in the morality or cultural lag between the thinking and values of life of the people and the power they have acquired due to the progress of modern science and technology. Several eminent persons and thinkers have drawn attention to it. Bertrand Russell has said: "The advance in the last five centuries has been greater than that in all previous recorded history. One of the troubles of our age is that habit of thought cannot change as quickly as techniques with the result that, as skill increases, wisdom fades."[4] General Omar N. Bradley indicated towards it in a more telling manner when he said: "The world has achieved brilliance without wisdom, power without conscience. Ours is the world of nuclear giants and ethical infants. We know more about war than we know about peace, more about killing than we know about living."[5] As an army person, Bradley's anxiety was probably about the danger of a nuclear war in the world with which I will deal later, but the cultural gap which he noted is much more comprehensive in extent. Arnold Toynbee writes: "Technology gives us material power, and this is morally neutral; it can be used, at will, for either good or ill. The greater our material power, the greater our need for spiritual insight and virtue to use our power for good and not for evil. Material power that is not counter-balanced by adequate spiritual power, that is by love and wisdom, is a curse not a blessing."[6] He had also pointed out that the increase in material wealth due to the application of science and technology has been unequally distributed and hence this success, so far from ensuring human happiness, has actually not increased it.[7]

The economic inequality referred to by Toynbee existed even in the past but the Industrial Revolution has widened the gap and it was this that gave birth to Marxism which thought of its remedy more in terms of social transformation than the transformation of man. In the past ages when the gap was not very wide, sages accorded importance to the transformation of man. The fate of Marxism in the Soviet Union and Eastern Europe highlights the need of the transformation of man as well, and we find a synthesis of the two transformations in Gandhian thought, with some priority to the transformation of man. Vinoba said: "The importance of changing the social structure is not denied. But it should be brought about through the development of particular moral attributes. There are certain abiding values and standards. If in a hurry to set up a particular type of social structure, these values and standards are lost, it will be tantamount to losing the capital in the avaricious bid for interest." And he further added: "It is no good of making a fetish of social reconstruction. After all, it is the people who construct a society. Hence the society will be as the individuals making it are. Hence, any scheme of changing the society must be not only subject to the preservation — indeed, enhancement — of standards of character and moral values, but the change must [also] be brought about by the means and strength of character and moral values. We must not worry if it takes place gradually and at seemingly lower pace . . . the slow pace will in the end prove itself to be the speediest."[8] Vinobaji's view on priority is supported by Pitrim A. Sorokin, an eminent sociologist, who says: "The transformation should be carried on simultaneously along all the three fronts: personal, cultural and social. The effortful transmutation of the individual may slightly precede the others."[9]

Vinobaji's statement clearly shows that he would not like the imposition of any social transformation by force on the people, since, besides being harmful in many ways, anything imposed by violence cannot prove abiding. Arnold Toynbee too is of the same view. He says: "History shows that violent revolutions in the past have almost always provoked a violent reaction. This either takes the form of a re-establishment of the pre-revolutionary regime in a rather more pleasant form than before, or it takes the still more ironical form of the conversion of the revolutionary regime itself into a caricature of the pre-revolutionary regime."[10] Toynbee is, in a way, seconded by Bart de Ligt who says that "greater the violence, the weaker the revolution."[11]

However, all eminent thinkers are of the view that for raising the living standard of the common people, industrialism is a must. Hence it is necessary to remove a misunderstanding about the Gandhian thinking on industrialism. Gandhiji was for some large-scale industries but he wanted them to be under state control,[12] while Vinobaji, as already mentioned in the earlier chapter, did not consider industrialism to be a curse and held that it had some good points which would have to be absorbed before it could be displaced. Gandhian thinkers are at least as anxious, if not more, to raise the living conditions of the poor as Marx was.

Now a few words about the danger of a nuclear war which must have been uppermost in the mind of General Bradley when he made his statement cited above in November 1948. The General had not been alone in having that fear. All thinking persons had been worried over it. But the development of atomic bomb by several countries and the realization that any atomic war would not be one-sided affair, made that danger recede. However, further acquisition or development of it by some other countries not recognized as nuclear powers has again raised the fears of at least local atomic wars.

But a third kind of danger of its use is certainly emerging, and it is by Islamic terrorists. There are reports that some nuclear scientists have passed the technology to them and though they may not be in a position to make sophisticated atomic bombs, they can certainly make crude bombs capable of causing terrible havoc. The experience of the 9/11 attack in the USA has made the people all the more alive to its danger. Hence the problem how to tackle them?

If we take into account the Indian experience, there are two main groups of terrorists, the Islamic and the Maoist or Naxalite. The second kind of terrorism is an extension of Marxism born of all kinds of atrocities and injustices perpetrated on the poorer sections of society by those who are generally both socially and economically higher to them and by government servants with whom they have to deal. Both Gandhians and Marxists can well cooperate with each other in dealing with them by taking up their struggle against injustices which can be looked upon as an extension of the previous national liberation movement. Vinobaji had once said: "Both Gandhism and Communism regard the well-being of the poor and the oppressed with the intensely loving regard of the mother. It often happens, however, that the infatuation to see immediate results gets the fond mother involved in entanglements of indiscretions, which makes her overlook the far-reaching results of her methods upon the child. This has happened to Communism."[13] And hence when once asked if there could be any compromise and cooperation between the two in the matter, his reply was: " There cannot be any compromise between the two, but there could be a good deal of cooperation. Sarvodaya will not give up its ideas because it is no reaction to any ideology. It is in itself a philosophy of life."[14]

It may be mentioned here that the world-acclaimed Bhoodan movement of Vinobaji was a response to the peasant struggle in Telangana. Though it did not succeed much in its objective, it was able to build up enough public opinion for the cause of the landless agricultural labourer. President Dr S. Radhakrishnan had observed at a seminar: "The cause of delay in the progress of the Bhoodan movement are those people who are at present in control of the Government."[15] P.B Gajendragadkar, a former Chief Justice of India is also reported to have said to Vinobaji: "Feelings in favour of it had been generated. Had the Government possessed imagination, it could have enacted a law on the basis of the atmosphere generated by you, and a revolution would have been achieved. But the Government did not do so and it is incapable of it."[16]

The moment terrorism is termed Islamic terrorism because its membership comes from the Muslim communities and it claims to be based on the teachings of Islam, it is a matter of controversy since many Muslims disagree with them on it. It primarily owes much of its strength to the money and weapons supplied to it by a great power keen to use it as an instrument of its dominance, politically and economically, in the Middle East. It forgot then that it was a dangerous policy to encourage religious fundamentalism wedded to violence since devouring their own children, it could also prove its enemy. It is a lesson which all who support it, should take to their hearts.

As regards dealing with it, Marxism which is anti-religious, has no answer to it except that of force. But Gandhian thought has an answer. It is no enemy of religion and has great regard for Prophet Mohammad. It believes in the equality of all religions and finds that common elements of spirituality and ethics run through them all.[17] In this matter, they have the support of Arnold Toynbee, who says that he would "express his personal belief that the four higher religions that were alive in the age in which he was living were four variations on the single theme, and that, if all the four components of this heavenly music of the spheres could be audible on the earth simultaneously, and with equal clarity, to one pair of human ears, the happy hearer would find himself listening, not to a discord, but to a harmony."[18] The same idea has also been expressed by Dr S. Radhakrishnan when he says: "When we go behind the dogmas and creeds and get down to the depth, we discover that all religions draw their strength from the same unfathomable source."[19] It may be expected that the fact of the absence of any real difference between the higher religions would, sooner or later, dawn upon the followers of all religions and they would come to have equal regard for all religions without any claim of superiority for their own religion. That is the only solution to prevent any clash of civilizations which appears to be inevitable to many. The idea of religious conversion is a corollary of the notion of superiority for one's religion, and that was also a reason why Gandhiji was opposed to it. It may also be mentioned here that Islamic terrorism also draws its nourishment from the sense of injustice which, rightly or wrongly, it harbours. It too has to be removed to the extent it is real.

To resume the thread of the problem of war, though the chances of a nuclear war in near future have receded, one cannot be sure of it. Moreover, even non-nuclear wars are now capable of causing enormous destruction of men and property. Hence, the need to minimize the possibility of wars to the maximum. The factors behind wars are both psychological and sociological. Referring to the first, Bertrand Russell has been of the view that the forces on the side of life are love, the instinct of constructiveness and the joy of life. But all these forces have been enfeebled.[20] Our institutions rest upon injustice and authority. The conventional conception of success and the present economic system with its over-emphasis on the material aspects of life and on competition, run counter to a life of love. They generate envy, hatred and selfishness. The modern system of production kills the instinct of creativeness by depriving the worker of opportunities for creative self-expression. And man is so constituted that if there is a lack of creative outlet, he would take pleasure in negative creation or destruction, Lastly, the present-day worker does not feel any joy in life. He has to work hard for his living and the desire for ever rising standard of living makes him work harder still when he hates his work. The result is that a large number of workers hate their jobs. Therefore, Russell is of the view that a change is needed both in the economic system and philosophy of life. Elaborating on the need of a philosophy of life, he says: "The world has need of a philosophy, or a religion, which will promote life. And in order to promote life it is necessary to value something other than mere life. . . . If life is to be fully human, it must serve some end which seems, in some sense, outside human life, some end which is impersonal, and above mankind, such as god or truth or beauty. Those who best promote life do not have life for their purpose."[21]

I have indicated above how Gandhiji's thinking on war has the support of some great thinkers of the last century. They need not agree with Gandhiji in toto but the trend of their thinking is very much the same. Gandhiji did not want to leave any creed behind him and his own thinking had been evolving. Marx was a product of the 19th century. These thinkers represent the last century and they are more relevant than Marx.

Thus practically on all points, the Gandhian thought has been found to be more capable of meeting the challenges facing the global community today. It is probably on considering all such issues that Ramashray Roy says politely about Gandhiji that though the issue of modernization has tended to relegate him and his teachings into the backwaters of history, the deepening crisis of modern civilization forces one to contemplate on the factors responsible for the crisis and the way to resolve it. And then he adds: "In the face of staring disaster, Gandhi inescapably comes to mind as one of the several thinkers whose counsel must be sought."[22] Vinoba too can be consulted since he took Gandhiji as an idea and set an example of interpreting him creatively in the post-war conditions which we face today.

NOTES AND REFERENCES

1. *Gandhi Marg,* July 1972, p. 212.
   The above issue of *Gandhi Marg* gives the report of the Secretary General to the United Nations in an abridged form.
2. ibid., pp. 222-23 and 225-26.
3. ibid., p. 213.

4. Bertrand Russell, *Has Man A Future?* (Allen & Unwin, London, 1961), p. 11.
5. Cited in Buddhadeva Bhattacharyya, *Evolution of the Political Philosophy of Gandhi* (Calcutta Book House, Calcutta, 1969), p. 282.
6. Arnold J. Toynbee, *Surviving the Future* (Oxford University Press, London, 1971),p. 41.
7. ibid., p. 31.
8. Introduction to K.G. Mashruwala, *Gandhi and Marx* (Navajivan, Ahmedabad, 1951), pp. 11-12.
9. Pitrim A. Sorokin, *Reconstruction of Humanity* (Bharatiya Vidya Bhavan, Bombay, 1958), p. 209.
10. Toynbee, op. cit., pp. 19-20.
11. G.N. Dhawan, *The Political Philosophy of Mahatma Gandhi* (Navajivan, Ahmedabad, 1962), p. 277.
12. *Harijan*, September 1, 1946, p. 225.
13. Introduction to Mashruwala, op. cit., pp. 29-30.
14. Vishwanath Tandon (ed), *Selections from Vinoba* (National Gandhi Museum, New Delhi, 2004), pp. 29-30.
15. *Vinoba Ka Vihar Parva* (Paramdham Prakashan, Paunar, 1998), p. 196.
16. ibid.
17. Vinobaji had been laying stress on it in many of his speeches.
18. Cited in S. Radhakrishnan, *East and West: Some Reflections* (Allen & Unwin, London, 1955), p. 128.
19. S. Radhakirishnan, *Religion and Society* (Allen & Unwin, London, 1948), p. 54.
20. Bertrand Russell, *Principles of Social Reconstructions* (Allen & Unwin, London, 1950), p. 23.
    I have discussed this question at some length in my *The Social and Political Philosophy of Sarvodaya After Gandhi* (Sarva Seva Sangh Prakashan, Varanasi, 1965) on the basis of the above book of Russell, Erich Fromm's *The Sane Society*, Lewis Mumford's *The Condition of Man* and M.A. Eliot and P.P. Merrik's *Social Disorganisation.*
21. Russell, op. cit., p. 245.
22. His article on *Gandhi and Our Times* in his edited book *Contemporary Crisis and Gandhi* (Discovery Publishing House, Delhi, 1986), p. 5.

PART TWO

Two Lectures of Vinoba (1941)

CHAPTER SIX

A Commentary on Three Main Ideologies

I addressed a meeting some time back and I presume that most of you must have heard me then. I had then expressed an idea of mine which I had also been repeating elsewhere in the same words. The reason for it has been that it is deeply implanted in my mind in that very language. According to it, only the students are entitled to an inviolable and uncontrolled right of full freedom of thought. Others have restraints which are justified. But the students should be totally free of them. If this right has not been conceded to them so far, let it be done from today. Being a student implies a (special) status and I am speaking here keeping this fact in my mind. However, I am not treating them as 'individuals'. As individuals, there may well be some restraints on them, but as one scrutinizing some idea or searching truth, they must enjoy the full status of being mere students. You should not accept anything because it is taught by a Mahatma, a *guru* or a saint. Full

---

This speech was originally delivered in Marathi at Wardha in December 1941 and was reported in *Sarvodaya*, the Hindi monthly of the Gandhi Seva Sangh. Here it has been translated in English with some editing, leaving out in particular some preliminary remarks of Vinoba, giving out the reason for his speaking in Marathi instead of Hindi as requested by a person in the audience.

freedom of thought is your right, an important fundamental right. If you yourselves remain unmindful of it or allow it to be violated, there would be no hope of your acquiring true education.

These days Germany, Russia and other 'civilized' countries have deprived the students of this basic right of theirs on the pretence of teaching them history, culture, commerce, geography etc. Frivolous sculptors of these days forget that Ganesh or Ganapati signifies some principles and while sculpting his figures, they forget it and follow their own whims. Some give *trishul* or spear in his hand, some a spinning wheel and some even present him smoking a cigarette. That is how he is being ridiculed. The same is going to happen with students. Intelligent students had never accepted it and it is the same with them these days. You should never be prepared to put up with such a pitiable state of affairs. What is happening in Germany? It is the Government which decides what would be taught to them, in what mould they would be cast and the teachers are its instruments for it. The educational schemes are drawn up on the basis of the desirability conception of the government. If you tolerate these atrocities, it will adversely affect you, us and the world. Capitalist countries draw up such schemes. It is the duty of students to oppose them fully.

This is the first thing I wanted to say. Its realization had compelled a sage to say: "My beloved pupils, you have been with me for twelve years, but do not take me as your ideal. Let the truth be your authority, not my words and actions. Test them on the touchstone of truth. Only accept that which stands examination. Reject those which do not stand it. The test for truth is readily available to the intelligent mind of everyone. Make use of it." He could say all this because he was a true giver of knowledge. What he said was nothing new, but it is not followed. Hence he delivered that message to his pupils out of his extreme kind heartedness towards them. You too should keep it well in mind. Preserve your fundamental right of the freedom of thought intact. Do not lose it.

As I have said, an independent mind is the first and the main trait of a student. By 'an independent mind', I denote a mind which is free of all pressures. That is also the mind of a satyagrahi. If you look at the world with such a mind, you will find innumerable surprising things taking place. Try to understand them intellectually. There is no place for a vacuous mind in this age. If you would not have strong and definite ideas of your own, those of others would lodge themselves in your brains. The world of today tells you not to have an empty mind. It must be filled with something. Let it be with noble thoughts. If you do not like it, stuff it with anything possible. The age will not allow it to remain empty. If you do not think for yourself, the radio will stuff your mind with its ideas. The newspapers compel one to think for himself. An empty mind is an impossibility. Hence have a mind of a Satyagrahi. Entertain noble ideas. The only choice before you is to nourish and strengthen them. Do not permit others to mould you.

It is impossible to remain indifferent in today's world. There is no place in it for any study in solitude, cutting oneself off from society. There is no alternative to studying sociology and its ideas. It is a must for any study of other subjects, be it history, commerce, political science, economics or even subjects like ethics, mathematics, general science, physics or any other, as if they are all offshoots of sociology. Therefore, it is absolutely essential for one to think constructively, keeping one's mind ever alert.

There are three important currents of thought in the world today. The first is Fascism and Nazism. They are essentially one. One was born in Germany and the other in Italy. They are found all over the world in one form or another, including India. The second is that of Communism which includes socialist thinking (in all its forms). This thought was first acted upon in Russia and then spread all over the world. The third is the thought of Mahatma Gandhi. These three thought currents are the only real ones. The thoughts prevalent in England, the U.S.A. and elsewhere do not count at all. They belong to the fraternity of Fascism and Nazism. No matter which of them gains an upper hand, they have no value as an ideology. They are bound to disappear ultimately. Its victory will be like the last flicker of a lamp going out.

The development of these ideologies is before us and it needs an objective study. Of these, Gandhism is almost an Indian development. I use the word 'almost' since there had been thinkers in other lands who expressed similar ideas. Some even acted upon them in ancient times. However, it is only in India that Gandhi gave these principles a material form and experimented with them in a tangible way on a national scale. Therefore, no objection can be raised against the word 'almost'. The conditions and the environment in India were favourable to his experiments.

The other two ideologies, Communism and Nazism, were born in Europe and we have to think why it so happened. A maxim formed by me is "*Indraya Takshakaya swaha*". Due to some quarrel with the serpents, a Brahmin held a *yajna*, sacrifice, in which the offerings were of serpents. Many serpents were given in oblations, but Takshak, a serpent, hid itself under the seat of Lord Indra and when the Brahmin gave a call for its oblation, there was no trace of it. He then surveyed the celestial world with his keen vision and found that his call had failed to materialize since Takshak had taken shelter with Indra. He then insolently called for the oblation of both Indra and Takshak together without taking the trouble of separating them. But since there could be no oblation of Indra due to his immortality, Takshak too became immortal with him.

There is no ideology without some merit. If we denounce an ideology wholesale and reject its good points, it becomes immortal (gets life). If its good and bad points are not separated, it thrives in spite of its defects. Therefore, it is essential to find out its good points. If Nazism is condemned totally, it gets strong and prospers. No ideology can be demolished by simply looking at its defects.

If we assimilate whatever is good in it, there is nothing left in that ideology to make it lasting. With this in view, we should try to discover the good in Nazism. It is based on a sense of pride in its old traditions and past history. Its thinking runs like this: "We, the Germans, are superior to others. We have a magnificent past. Therefore the Supreme Being or Destiny has entrusted to us an important mission. We can only fulfill it by preserving and fostering our ancient culture. Hence we should maintain the purity of our race. We have been entrusted with the mission because of our superior qualities. Individuals too, like societies and nations, possess special qualities. In them lies their uniqueness, their peculiarity. Our culture is pure. Only we Germans with our pure blood, lineage and thinking can fulfill that mission. Purity here stands for what has been traditionally acquired. Just as the qualities inherited by frogs, serpents, lions etc. are pure for them, the special traditional qualities of the culture inherited by us, are pure for us. Therefore, we must preserve our traditions by having pride in our race."

Nazism may have several defects but this feature of it is greatly alluring. Yet, it cannot be fully acceptable to us. What is really worth accepting in it is its advocacy for maintaining the continuity of traditions without break and for having respect and attachment for the culture of one's forefathers. But the racial pride found in it is not worth preserving.

On the other hand, Communism has a different merit. It finds that while the poor of the world are getting poorer and poorer, the rich are getting richer and richer. The depth of the empty stomachs of the poor has increased and acquired the depth of the Pacific Ocean, while the pile of the wealth with the rich has acquired the height of the Himalayas. Communism was born since this disparity became intolerable. According to it, the majority-based polity of today is not true democracy. Counting of heads does not imply it since the heads of the poor are controlled by the rich and their votes signify nothing. There can be no equality of rights for all unless the rich are extirpated. The present system of franchise gives it only an appearance of democracy. The Communists say that they want to establish a polity with the qualities of a real democracy and not merely its form. It would be a democracy without any feeling of partiality. Impartiality under the present situation demands favouring of the poor. So far, we have raised the prestige of the rich in the name of equal rights and played farce with the concepts of equality, justice and equal opportunities. The last has only meant the grinding of the poor. It has been like making a powerful wrestler fight a lean and thin opponent, in which the former was sure to win. First liberate the poor and then talk of the equality of opportunities. All kinds of means can be used for their liberation. There would be nothing wrong about it. Thus the merit of Communism lies in its extreme stand in favour of the poor.

That is how these two ideologies are spreading here and in other parts of the world due to their good points. They are keen to spread in Maharashtra too which I am here referring to in particular since if I point out the defects of my own province, there can be no misunderstanding about it. Such phrases as "Maharashtra Dharma", "the rule of the Peshwas", "our Maratha soldier", "Our Samartha (Guru Ramadas)" etc. attract its youth since they excite emotions in them. It is also due to it that they prefer the ideas of the Hindu Mahasabha in which they find the great quality of pride in ancient history. The observations of such days as Dasnavami, Hanuman Jayanti, Shivaji Utsava, etc. inspire and agitate them. Hence, in spite of their defects, the youth find them alluring. These celebrations have the merit of pride in old traditions (and history).

The Muslim League is also propagating similar ideas among the Muslims by talking to them of the past splendour of Islam, its rule over this country and such other things. Therein lies its merit of pride in its past traditions (and history). Such actions of the Hindu Mahasabha and the League create a likeness between them and the Nazis. They even admit it when talking frankly. Otherwise, they do not refer to it at all. However, they are sympathetic towards the Nazis. Some of their special features like the green flag of the League or that of the Mahasabha with the figure of Hanuman on it and their special ways of oath-taking point to their similarities with the Nazis. Those who attend their functions get inspired with zeal and acquire a feeling that they are not being misled by them on a totally wrong path.

The poverty of India is like the Brahma of the Upanishads, incomparable or one without a second. This has made Communism with its profession in the good of the poor and its animosity towards the rich, attractive and led to its spread.

Thus these two ideologies, Nazism and Communism, have proved alluring for different reasons. The factor working in favour of Nazism is its pride in the ancient traditions preached by it, while the poverty of the common people makes Communism acceptable. However, these comments on them here are not meant to point out their defects but to discover their strong points.

Now I take up the third ideology advocated by Gandhiji. We should understand it well. Some have the feeling, what can a physically weak Gujarati do in this field? The Gujaratis are cowards, harmless like cows, disinclined even to kill snakes, only interested in business and nothing else. They have never wielded swords. Their tradition is only of weakness and any ideology emanating from them can only appeal to similar people. But I may tell you that it is not so. Had it been weak and cowardly, I would have long rejected it as a Maharashtrian. I would never commend any weak ideology, no matter what be its nature. But, as I have said, it is not really so and you can well examine it for yourselves. If you don't do it, I will only say that you students are getting dull. That's the only adjective I will use for you.

Since a century and a half, Indians have been a disarmed people. They have been lacking both in the power of arms and that of wealth. Hence the question facing such a powerless country was how to acquire power not to bend before others. Was it possible to do so while keeping to our traditions? This led to a churning of thought how to make the four hundred million people strong to stand erect.

Some were of the view that they should copy the West and learn from them. Some felt that a reform of religion could uplift us and with this in view Brahma Samaj, Prarthana Samaj, Arya Samaj, Theosophical Society, etc. were established. They may appear to be religious organizations but the motive behind them was different. It was how could the country, in the absence of the powers of arms and wealth, stand erect on the basis of the power of intellect? To attain it, educational reforms were undertaken since therein only lay the hope. That is why in the period prior to that of Gandhiji, religious reforms were linked to educational reforms. Raja Rammohan Roy, Swami Dayanand, Devendranath Tagore, Rabindranath Tagore, Sri Aurobindo and other great souls attempted to uplift people on the basis of intellect. What else could they do when neither the power of arms nor that of the wealth was there?

For reforms in education, they followed the English educational system. This gave rise to another view that "we don't need to worship the English system. Give the present system a new form imparting a momentum to the ancient system." This led to the establishment of Gurukuls and such other institutions giving birth, in turn, to the movement for national education. It was an attempt to reap the benefits of both the Sanskrit learning and the new learning. It was held that national education implied both revival and reform. However all these ideas were based on the notion of empowerment through intellectual development. There are three gateways to empowerment — arms, wealth and intellect. When the first two were closed for fighting the British, the third was the only option left. It was due to it that the movement for national education had been started. Many reformers had participated in it.

But how to empower the intellect? Would it only suffice in itself? Could an intellect unaccompanied by actions get powerful? The answer to it could only be in the negative. And with this realization, the Congress was founded. Prior to that, the thinking favoured simply the use of intellect for the removal of the grievances of the people. But the method of representing the grievances for removal had its limitations. It did not succeed fully. It only brought the unnoticed grievances into limelight. These intellectual efforts needed to be joined with actions to succeed. That is why the submission of grievances by the Congress too (in its earlier stages) did not prove effective. The reason for it was that it did not strike at the root cause of those grievances, which lay in the country's political slavery.

The Congress, as was natural, realized it afterwards. While a person may hew down all the branches of a tree, he cannot do it with the branch on which he is standing. The British Government could carry out several reforms but how could it be expected to strike at the branch on which its authority rested? All rational appeals were bound to fail when they came to it.

The people came to understand it. But the question was how to compel the government for it and what to do about it? It was realized then that it required empowerment and that all efforts need some devices or strategies, and the method they then adopted was of working secretly. In other words, the idea of making bombs and killing officers entered their heads. Some officers were even murdered. All this was done out of pure (selfless) motives. I am myself among those who revere the memory of those persons who adopted that method. But what was their experience? It was that they required funds to make bombs. Shivaji had also to take to the method of conspiracy and to loot Surat for funds. The Marathas had to commit docoities in Bengal. Now these revolutionaries had to do the same, though out of pure motives and on the basis of the teaching of the *Gita*. However, the professional dacoits of the times, with their better expertise, committed many more dacoities and it was not possible for the people to distinguish between the two. How could a he-goat distinguish whether the knife used for killing it was that of a butcher or of the Brahmin. The people failed to distinguish between the two and cried for protection. It suited the government. Thus their method failed since the people failed to distinguish the anarchists from the dacoits.

Then came Mahatma Gandhi. He said: "The objective of the anarchists is correct but not their methods. The objective is correct because the branch supporting India's slavery has to be hewed down, but their violent methods cannot suit the country." As a matter of fact, they cannot prove suitable anywhere. They need for success highly organized violence used on a wide scale. The governments of today are highly organized and based on the utmost pervasive violence, which cannot be matched by the people. Hence their violence can be of no avail against the government and it would fail to build up the power of the people. What it can at the best do is to satisfy the longing to do something for the country and it does so without in anyway helping them in organizing the people. It proves ineffective from the viewpoint of uplifting the country.

It was because of it that Gandhi said: "My method of openly organizing the people will prove effective. The basis of a government does not lie in any authority it possesses inherently but in the authority conceded to it by the people (for its maintenance). Both hands are needed to clap and in this case the two hands are the government and the people. If you withdraw your hand, its hand will automatically get relaxed. If the people withdraw the authority they have handed over to the government, it would not last. It is by an open organization of the people that the power of resistance can be developed in them."

How could India become a nation of four hundred millions? It has been due to the virtues of our old traditions. It is not a small nation. In the words of our highly respected national poet, Rabindranath Tagore, "*Aiyee Bharater mahamanaver sagarateere*". Peoples from all over the world came and settled here. Not all of them did so forcibly by invading the country. We provided them place to settle after weighing all aspects of it as in the case of Parsis (Zoroastrians) who had not invaded the country. It has been an old tradition of this country to help others but not to invade other countries.

This tradition inspired Gandhi to think that we have a weapon of resistance with us. The word *shastra*, used for arms or weapons, really means that which rules or regulates life. Hands fall in this category, but not weapons which are mere instruments devoid of any consciousness of their own. They have no independent existence and they are also not needed.

This idea was born as a historical demand to fulfill a dire need of this country. That is why it could spread. While elsewhere in the world nonviolence is not even talked about, here even the youth discuss if in our national dealings there has been an increase of violence or nonviolence. We do not say that all should become nonviolent immediately, but all must certainly think over it. The fact that the youth today have now started thinking anew on nonviolence, is indicative of real progress. It was not possible for Gandhi's idea to spread more rapidly and it was good that it did not. It should be adopted gradually, after proper consideration and understanding.

I will like to ask you if this idea of nonviolent resistance was not born of our old tradition — the main old tradition and not the various sundry ones like those of the Marathas, the Rajputs, the Sikhs, etc. The main tradition is that which unites the peoples of various religions, sects and races. This idea is its product and we should be proud of that tradition.

Thus even the good element in Nazism is in consonance with it. We used to discuss it while in prison, taking into consideration the condition of the country and of this region (Maharashtra), and the life and activities of all those individuals who brought about revolutionary changes in Indian history, right from the Vedic times to the present age, irrespective of the race or religion they belonged to. Within this tradition that of the Marathas occupies such a petty place and that of the Brahmins is so insignificant that they need not be taken into consideration separately. The tradition of India is like a big banyan tree. It would not be a matter of any lofty pride to cut down its branches and to break our heads instead of taking shelter under it. The tradition of India is that of the authors of religious treatises and of innumerable saints, be they Hindus, Muslims, Sikhs or any other, and also that of its various regions like Bengal, Maharashtra, Gujarat or any other. And I have not the least doubt that if I give up this tradition, I would be depriving the country of its glory and incapacitating it for any creative work.

However, while Gandhism shares with Nazism its pride in old traditions, its nature is so different that it does not have the defect of the racial arrogance found in Nazism. Its tradition has a broad outlook and hence its pride is almost cosmopolitan. Moreover, a scrutiny of that tradition also goes on along with its continuity. Thus while resembling Nazism in its pride for its old traditions and its attractiveness, it is free of the narrowness of its racial arrogance. Really speaking, the word 'pride' hardly fits it when its chief feature has been a scrutiny of its ancient cultural efforts (ideas).

When some Communists say that the poor have to be liberated from their sufferings, they use a wrong language. The feeling underlying it is that they are their deliverers and as such they are different from them. It is only the poor who can liberate themselves and Gandhi made them capable of it. What could not be done in Russia, cannot be done here. The opportunities available there, are not (even) available here. And they are also not needed since the method adopted there does not lead to people's empowerment, it is the poor themselves who must liberate themselves and therein also lies the essence of Communism. We have absorbed this essence of it in the manner we assimilate the nourishing elements of almonds and milk. We have to separate the essentials from the non-essentials in Communism, accepting the former while rejecting the latter.

Communism envisages a revolution through violence. It is an essential part of it. The power of violence can never be of the people, and it is the same with the power of intellect which had been looked upon as that of a handful of Brahmins (intellectuals). It remained under their lock and key. The sword power too does not belong to the people which includes the old, women, children and others physically weak. It suits only the physically strong and there is no guarantee that they would always be noble-minded. And, then, their power too is temporary. Whatever is attained by violence can only be retained by it. This explains its incapacity to become the power of the poor or the common people.

Germany's invasion of Russia cannot be morally supported but it can be justified on the ground of realism. The military expenditure of Russia was 1600 crore (rupees) yearly, and Germany could not be so foolish as to allow its strong military force to grow (further) powerful in times of peace. Why was Russia increasing its military strength? Was it to worship as deities its men in military uniforms? It spent so much money on it because it is bent upon establishing Communism in the world through violence. It was not in Germany's interest to allow the Communist ideology to spread and flourish. Therefore it appeared rational to it to destroy the power of Russia.

From the viewpoint of England, wisdom lay in deriving benefit from Russia's power. It says: "Let us face Germany now by using the military might of Russia. We will see to it later." Russia urges the US, "We have not at all attempted to abolish religions. You can help us." Thus, in other words, Russia is being compelled to flatter hypocrites. What does all this mean? It only shows its dependence on others. Will it then be able to save Communism? Will it enable it to avoid military authoritarianism? Even if it emerges victorious out of the war with the help of countries which are either non-Communists or standing for inequalities, it will not save Communism, while a defeat will lead to its death. What is not possible for Russia or any other country in the world, how can it be possible for India? People's power does not lie in violence. Let us make people courageous and strong.

We have absorbed the essence of Communism, its belief in making the people capable of uplifting and liberating themselves, while rejecting the non-essentials in it. We have also accepted the call of Nazism for a healthy pride in old traditions while preserving along with it our another tradition of its continuous scrutiny. However, the word 'pride' does not express it correctly because of its broad outlook. The pride in old traditions in a homogenous country is (likely to be) narrow, while the tradition of India is mixed and broad. Because of it being a heterogeneous country, its pride in its old traditions can never be narrow. It is without any blemish.

I have thus explained to you the third ideology with as much objectivity as possible, an ideology which combines in itself the good points of the other two, namely a broad-minded pride in the traditions of this country and an effort to develop the latent power of the people. The reason for using the words 'with as much objectivity as possible' is that as a believer in that ideology and as one who has made a part of his life, I am, in a sense, a partisan. But then you have to keep in mind the principle enunciated by me earlier, asking you not to accept a thing because I or Gandhi says it but to think over it objectively, taking a comprehensive view of the whole matter.

I have already explained to you that violence cannot be the power of the people. But it remains to explain how nonviolence can be their power or, in other words, how it can be made a social force. There are individual examples of its successful use both in India and elsewhere. Saint Ekanath, Christ and Socrates have demonstrated its capability by their strict adherence to it. That is how experiments are conducted. Individual scientists experiment first in laboratories. After verification there, the principles are applied on a bigger scale in society. The steam power was discovered by an individual on observing its effect on a tea kettle. Later it was made use of in society. If that discovery had remained confined to an individual, it would not have been of any avail. However, it is not so with individual experiments in nonviolence. They too give results. But if applied socially, they do a lot.

Doubts are, however, expressed if a whole society can be turned into Ekanaths, Christs and Buddhas. Had there been any such possibility, there would have been no need to put forward any scheme for it before you. The people like us can derive benefits from their experiments. We do not need their (extraordinary) talent for it. Newton did need special intelligence to discover the law of gravity but a technician making use of that power does not need that much of it. Even Hitler has no rival in his field. He may be inventing newer and newer weapons, but the intelligence he needs for it is not required of the soldier using them. The first inventor or discoverer has to be a genius but for any social application of the discovery or invention that phenomenal intelligence is not required. It was required of Gandhi to be a genius since without it he could not have discovered the method of nonviolent resistance. But no such super-normal talent is needed for its social application.

Take the example of multiplication. *Takli* is a very small instrument. Some fifty metres of spun yarn can only be winded up on it at one time. But if forty crores of people spin on it, the yarn spun will get multiplied by that number. The same is with nonviolence. It is also simple, small and convenient like a *takli*. It can be used by all—women, children and old people. A spinning factory needs (several) horsepower of energy which a *Takli* does not. The talents of Christ are not required for an application of nonviolence. Christ is like a spinning mill for its experiments, while we, the forty crore people, are *taklis* for its application. If we all develop a bit of nonviolence in us; it will prove of greater benefit to society than the nonviolence in Christ. It is of no benefit to use mounds of manure at one small place in a field but if it is scattered one inch deep throughout it, it proves of greater benefit. Similarly, if every one of us also develops nonviolence in us even in small amounts, we would achieve something loftier than the Himalayas and more effective than the vast amount of nonviolence Christ had.

CHAPTER SEVEN

Our Logical Role

I did not know that I had been invited here to do something which was within my domain. I realized it only after hearing what the Principal of the College said. He pointed out that the College was being shifted to Nagpur from the next session and it is the last session to be held here. I am often invited for closing speeches, as if I am only entitled to it. It is surprising how an appropriate person is automatically selected for a work. The people near me were surprised to see me accepting the invitation. They doubted my suitability for it. Jnanadeva has written that once a wild animal was brought to a noisy place bustling with activity. It was taken aback on reaching there. My fellow workers thought that my condition would be similar, since a college atmosphere differs from that of ours. Hence their doubts had some justification.

But I had no such fear, since a student, no matter however different he be, has the same disposition as I have. I look upon them as kindred souls. It has been my experience many a time

---

This speech of Vinoba was delivered before the students of Vasudeva College, Wardha on December 14, 1941. It originally appeared in *Sarvodaya*, the Hindi monthly of the Gandhi Seva Sangh in its January 1942 issue. It has been translated into English. Its importance lies in Vinobaji explaining Gandhiji's method of nonviolent resistance in terms of the dialectics used by Marx, and the allied issue of violence.

when I had to face them. When I speak to them, I never have the feeling that I am addressing different kinds of persons. I then feel that my own self has been personified in them and I am talking to myself. The reason is that I too am a student. Therefore, no matter how different the environment, when I am among them, I feel no distinction between them and myself. Having no doubt on this score, I accepted the invitation.

However, the problem pertaining to the topic of speech was there. Even then, I had the realization that they have invited me keeping in mind the work I had been engaged in and, therefore, I was quite clear as to what they wanted me to speak about and I am going to speak on it. But allow me to say one thing. According to the preliminary remarks (of the Principal), I am expected to deliver some sermon, but I am not going to do it. A maxim of my life has been that one who preaches any sermon to students, is a literate fool and one who listens to it is another such. As regards the characteristic of such a fool, you must be knowing what (Swami) Ramadasa has said about them. However, I find that such fools are now on the increase and the old statistics about them would not do.

When I say that preaching sermon to students signifies foolishness, I mean thereby that it is they in the world who are entitled to full, unrestrained liberty. Others always have to work under limitations born of fear, pressure, difficulties and restraints and it is not unreasonable. But a student should have no restraints imposed on him. I say it on the basis of my personal experience as one with the mentality of a student, and I would not myself accept any in that position. There are some restraints imposed on me as a citizen, as a son of my parents and as a fellow worker of others and my accepting them is a different matter. But it should be expected of a student that he would examine everything objectively and every subject should be dealt before him expecting the same of him. It is for him to decide what would be appropriate or inappropriate. Hence I will deliver no sermon.

The function of knowledge is that of a mirror which is objective and reflects a correct image. It would not however, cleanse the nose of anyone and it would not even persuade or force him to do so. It leaves it to his choice. A mother may even do it (in the case of her child). The mirror will only tell about it and it is able to do it because it itself is clean. There is no greater mistake in the process of the imparting of knowledge than to deliver sermons. This rule was followed by the authors of (our) *Shastras*, and that was why they could exercise control over our society and were called *Shastrakars*. Their method was to explain the situation correctly and then to leave the matter these. Following this rule of theirs I too will accept your right to judge for yourselves, and (with these remarks) I now come to what I have to say.

Since you are college students, you must be aware of the situation in the country and you must be knowing what is being said and written about it. Just look at the world as it is today. The whole of the mankind is feeling a severe labour pain, similar to the turmoils going on within the earth which result in earthquakes. It is not possible for anyone to predict what this pain experienced by mankind would lead to. It is such as had never been experienced during the last few centuries. The (known) history of the human race is believed to be some ten thousand years old, while the history books you read deal only with the last three thousand years or so. The history of two thousand years prior to this period is a matter of mere surmise. However, in fact, the history of the human society is at least a million years old. Therefore, the history we read only deals with the last part of the period of mankind. Many revolutionary changes must have taken place during this whole period, many abdominal pains experienced. However, during the known period of history, such a severe pain had not been felt earlier.

The whole world appears to have got involved in the present war. I am using here the expression 'the whole world' not in any symbolic or figurative sense. It is so literally and we should understand it well. The present war is a 'total war' involving the whole world. In other words, it is a war in which a whole nation is reckoned as an enemy by another, making all men and women of one country treat the men and women of another country as enemies. The same applies to animals, trees, tools and machineries. And this enmity is all-sided, expressed in every way with no legal rules applying to it, eliminating everything likely to stand in the way of victory. That is why I term it a 'total war'.

I read the other day that what England has now done is unprecedented in its history. It enacted a law on compulsory involvement, in the war, of all women above 18, whether unmarried or married but issueless. It was estimated that their number may come to some 1.6 millions. But even this was not considered satisfactory enough, and girls between 16 and 18 are also expected to associate themselves in war activities. It is said amongst us that a son above 16 should be treated as a 'friend'. Similarly, a girl over 16 is being treated there as capable of participating in war.

As against it, Russia has issued a different kind of order. It is reported that some one million soldiers have either been killed, wounded or taken prisoners in the war, incapacitating them from taking part in it. No matter how it may be calculated, out of a population of some 180 millions not more than 4.5 millions can be such as to be able to participate in the war, and all of them cannot be sent as combatants to the war front, since for every combatant three others are needed for various services pertaining to electricity, water, roads, manufacture of armaments etc. If the ratio of such men be taken as 1:3, not more than 1.5 million could serve as combatants, and of these some one million have been incapacitated for it (as said above). This clearly shows that they are experiencing shortage of male combatants. However, they are not prepared to accept defeat in the matter and they have declared imposition of tax on all married men and women without issues and on all singles of marriageable age. In other words, just as we try to increase production of tanks in case of their shortage, production of human beings for the purpose of dying is being encouraged to make up for their lack. It is not that they would be immediately available for the purpose, since it would take at least eighteen years to achieve it. No doubt, the loss of men has to be made up, even if it be later, and that is why their planning for the manufacture of human beings. How horrible it all is!

What would come out of this unpleasant situation. The people name this situation resulting from the abdominal pain as the construction of a 'new order'. The work of destruction they are engaged in presently is, from the philosophical viewpoint, the work of weeding out and they hope that as a result of this war, a new human society will emerge. Even taking it for granted that it would so happen, you have to think if we would accept what comes about by itself or we would like to have something definite to result in accordance with our planning. You have to ponder over it deeply. There is not the least doubt that the human society after the war would not be what it presently is.

It was easy to start the war for those who did it, but, as the war escalates, it is not they who are controlling it, it is the war which is controlling them. They are led by it. It is said that Hitler is most powerful and adept in planning. But the war going on today cannot be said to be doing so according to his plans. Whatever be its outcome, whatever be achieved after so much destruction and sacrifice, it would not be worth it all, despite something resulting from it.

Strange things follow terrible earthquakes. Sometimes the positions of the seas are changed and so also of the mountains. These far-reaching changes which occur because of them, are neither man-planned nor man-made even though they affect the life of human beings. They constitute (what may be termed) self-desired revolutions. If we can bring about the desired changes through the present war, we can treat it to be a planned one. Otherwise, changes are bound to come about by themselves. Was the purpose of all these killings to give a new shape to the world, no matter what it might be? Was not this terrible war started to obtain definite results according to some plans? But it is quite evident now that all persons reputed to be very strong — like Churchill, Hitler, Stalin and Roosevelt — have become its slaves. They have no control over it. On the other hand, it rather controls them. Their reins are in its hands. I am prepared to accept such a terrible war provided it leads to desired changes. Otherwise, we will have to accept whatever comes about. The present war is useless for any new (desirable) re-construction. It is not moving in the right direction. The reply of Lord Halifax pertaining to it reflects reality. Questioned about the aim of the war, he unintentionally admitted that its aim is victory, when earlier it has been declared that it was a war for democracy and so on. The cat is out of the bag now. What other aim could he have given? Are not wars started for the pleasure of victory or of fighting. All wars do have some objectives, but once they have begun, those objectives take back seats and the people starting it get entangled in them. They get out of control and such wars can never lead to any definite, desired and planned outcomes.

Hence the question, why should we join it? How far is it necessary for us to do so simply because some others have done so? Intelligent peoples not only of India but throughout the world should think over joining such a stupid war, and the only answer they would get to it would be that it would not be proper to do so. And once it is decided not to join it, the question arises if it would be proper to play the role of objective onlookers. The only answer an intelligent person can give to it is that the role of an objective observer will not be a correct one.

However, as college (grown-up) students who would be soon holding the reins of the world in your hands, you should objectively think over it and decide. Examine the validity of the view placed before you, forgetting for the time being that it is a very ferocious war. (If you agree with me), you will come to two conclusions. First, it would not be proper to join a war that has gone out of men's control. Secondly, it would not become of those who do not join it to be mere neutral onlookers of it when those who have joined it are moving towards dire destruction. This, however, raises the question what is to be done if we are not to sit silently. If you think over it, you would understand the usefulness or what is being done by some Congressmen. It is our duty to develop an attitude and mode of thought opposed to those which have been created by the launching of the war. This is the third conclusion at which we arrive.

Some may question: "What good would it do when all others have joined the war? What difference would it make if a handful of people like you take to resisting it?" My answer to it is: Are the first two conclusions then meaningless? Let us leave it to the future. Let us first decide what is our duty. Is it not to develop an anti-war role? Will it not have some effect? And why not? Let us first present before the people a dynamic thinking of an anti-war role. Why should we have any doubt on the power of thought and public opinion? I do not claim that the development of such a role would bring the war to an end. I have no such hope. But if intelligent people make their anti-war thinking strong and powerful, a front of thought power will be created which on the weakening or the end of the war will get revived and then it may be your responsibility to work for the reconstruction of a new society. Is it not for us to make preparations for it from this very day? Hence we must start doing it. However, when we do it, the Government declares that it would not allow it. But the building up of such a front seems to us to be our duty, since with the help of such a front we would be able to give to the world the desired direction after the war. Those who are mad after the war and steeped in it, have lost control over it and they cannot be expected to achieve any definite objective. Therefore, those intelligent people who do not want to get involved in the war, should build up a war-resistance role since those who are war intoxicated and steeped in it will find themselves tired physically and even more so mentally after the war for it. Hence your role should be such that they naturally feel compelled to adopt your path. And it is not a question of number. Those who have maintained their sanity will be entitled to provide guidance. It is they on whom will fall the responsibility to build up a society according to their plan. Hence their duty to build up an active role of anti-war thinking.

But who will allow us to do this work easily? The present rulers and managers would surely punish and suppress us if we try for it. But since doing so would amount to be an injustice to us, it would be our supreme duty to resist it. In short, after pondering on the causes of the commencement of the war, it will be our duty to build up such conditions as may work against them. Our first principle is that injustice must be resisted, and the second is that our mode of resistance would be unique in that it would be the one Gandhiji gave to the world. Had the world accepted his method of resistance, the scene in Europe would have been different today. The other day Ribbentropp claimed that now there is no danger of the disturbance of peace in Europe, since tanks are patrolling all places and the people have been disarmed. Those arrogant persons have learned it from the Britishers who having disarmed India thought that they were safe since they had weapons which Indian had not, and that they can (henceforth) safely rule despotically. This is what Ribbentropp also meant. It is the governing maxim of all such others, though there be slight differences. The strategy followed by all -- England, Russia, Japan and the USA — is to disarm people while equipping themselves with weaponry to the utmost.

Karl Marx has enunciated an important principle whose knowledge can make us realise the importance of the thought gifted by Gandhiji. You must be familiar with the name of Karl Marx and must have read his books. His theory is that if a thesis gets spread in the world, it leads both to some good and some harm. It is so under all systems, be it monarchy, capitalism or any other. However, it lasts only so long as it is more conducive to good than harm. But when it is otherwise, an anti-thesis comes to be propagated which assails the thesis, giving rise to a third element of synthesis which has the virtues of both. Take for instance the system of *varna-vyavastha*. It has both merits and demerits. Its merits lie in its ability to organize people of similar capabilities together and entrusting to them the work according to their special capabilities. That is what is termed as *varna-vyavastha*. Its de-merit is that it strengthens the feelings of high and low. This system, however, would last till its merit predominates over its demerit, but when the feelings of the high and the low and of the conflict of interests start getting strong, opposition to them by the element of oneness and equality gains force. Out of this conflict emerges a third element which combines the merits of the two in the manner of the grafting of lemon with *mausambi*, resulting in the production of *santra*, which is both sweet and sour. However, the process in society is not a planned one. It goes on by itself. As the latent defects of a system begin to appear, it gives birth to the opposing element (anti-thesis) and then to the birth of the third element (synthesis) by itself. Similarly, the new method of resistance (nonviolent) is a product of history according to the Marx's doctrine. Gandhiji was only an instrument of its expression.

The method followed so far has been that after defeating an armed people, one tried to become more united and equipped with arms. This gave rise to another practice of keeping the enemy (conquered) unarmed while keeping themselves well armed. Hence as a result of that situation the unarmed were made to think of this method of (nonviolent) resistance, and Gandhi is (only) an instrument for this insight. Had he not done so, someone else would have done it. If thirty or forty crores of people could be kept enslaved for ever, they must be lacking in human qualities. If it is not so, they must find some way to gain their freedom. Their distinguishing quality as a human being lies in its discovery. This whole theory (of thesis, anti-thesis and synthesis) is termed as 'dialectic', *vikartavada* in Hindi. The Hindi term signifies that its logic is something special and different from the ordinary logic. I have simply explained to you in short what has been termed as 'dialectic'.

Disarming a whole nation is a product of the brains of the peoples of the medieval age. It was a very risky experiment on the part of those who did it, taking upon themselves the responsibility of protecting those people. England disarmed India and now they must be realizing that it was not a wise thing on their part to do. It is due to it that they have now started saying, "Come and join the war, we will train you how to use weapons."

However, that ill-motivated experiment of theirs proved advantageous to us from one point of view. It has been due to it that we could discover the method of nonviolent resistance. Gandhi is only acting as a 'mouthpiece' of the Indian people. He has been impressing on them for the last twenty years of the importance of this weapon. The sword (weapon) has no independent power of its own. It is, after all, a mere piece of iron, stored up in the mines. It yet remains a piece of iron even if an artisan shapes it into a sword. Are the soil and an earthen vessel (fundamentally) different? A weapon is inanimate. At the back of it lies the animate power which gives it its strength. If it is not these, a sword or weapon would not work by itself. Its power depends on one who uses it. This fact was not realized earlier but circumstances led Gandhi to realize it.

A friend of mine is fond of relating an incident confirming the uselessness of a weapon in itself. Some thieves entered the house of a person. Seeing them, he lost his senses and started calling for his gun, which he was not even able to pronounce correctly. And even if he had a gun, of what use would it have been to him? The thieves could have certainly made use of it if they did not have their own with them.

It all amounts to saying that weapons do not work independently. Had we not been disarmed, this fact could not have occurred to us. Sages too are inspired to think and act by the conditions of their times. No doubt, Gandhiji had something special in him which led him to think of it, but the real reason for it lay in the condition of India.

We used this weapon (of nonviolent resistance), efficiently or inefficiently, for twenty years and our experience has been that though unarmed we can fight (for our independence) with it. But people ask, "What has been the result of it all?" My reply to it is: "You, who look for results, should exercise patience. You have experimented with violence for the last ten thousand years. Do you need to experiment further more with it? Do we not find that even after so many years, we are still compelled to use it? You allowed the believers of violence so much time and opportunity. Will you not allow us also time to experiment with nonviolence? And then you should also take into consideration the capability we have developed during the last twenty years in using it."

Discussions used to be held on this issue in the Nagpur Jail. The participants there were all satyagrahis with no believer in untruth. We were of the opinion then that if our 'showy' experiments (with nonviolence) could prove so effective, what a strong impact a 'real' thing would have. While experiments with violence extending over ten thousand years have been failures, our imperfect nonviolence of twenty years has proved quite effective in the field of resistance. Will we not be justified in entertaining further expectations from it? To say the least, while there are doubts about the efficacy of violence, one can expect nonviolence to achieve much.

Had Europe accepted the method of satyagraha, the situation there today would have been such as to make Hitler feel restless. He went on occupying one country after another but got enmeshed in Russia which is powerful. Even then, England did not dare to invade Germany from land. This surprised many since there could be no better opportunity for it. It only attempted to make a surprise attack on the German forces in Libya. In short, when a powerful and rich country like England finds it difficult to resist, what may other countries do (who are not powerful and rich)? And what can they do except to sit silently and submit before tanks? They cannot think of anything else.

But Gandhiji has given us a new weapon. A vow of resistance is only feasible on its basis. Such a vow taken on the strength of a sword will last only as long as it is in one's hand. On the other hand, the vow of resistance to injustice can always be observed by taking recourse to nonviolence, no matter what be the situation and whether the person be a man or a woman.

You should think over the whole situation with a calm mind. It is said that the people of Maharashtra are logical and rational. But had it been true, I would have rejoiced over it. (Really speaking), Maharashtra is imbued with an inert, *tamsi*, faith. I think that the old Marathi habits and the tradition of Nana Fadnavis are there in our blood. Brothers, the old teachings and tradition of Nana Fadnavis will prove of no avail in the altered times and circumstances of today. Nana is considered to have been a very wise person who therefore could save the Maratha kingdom with cleverness. His wisdom, however, lay in foreseeing that the British rule was going to stay in the country. They (the Maharashtrian people) argue that nonviolent methods are not in our blood, they are not a part of our thinking. But I am not prepared to accept that the method glorified by Namadeva, Tukaram and other (Maratha) saints is not in our blood. If it is so, we would become backward for all times and would never lead society. We would never rise if depending on the traditions of the Peshwas and Nana Fadnavis we refuse to move with times. On the other hand, if you learn the method which can make the weak strong and teach it to others, then after the war you will easily come to lead those who feel exhausted both physically and mentally because of it.

APPENDICES

1. Vinoba and the Theory of Trusteeship
2. Vinoba and Satyagraha
3. Bhoodan-Gramdan Movement (1951–74)—A Review

APPENDIX 1

Vinoba and the Theory of Trusteeship

During the lifetime of Gandhiji Indian intellectuals, particularly those who had Marxian leanings, had generally pooh-poohed his advocacy of economic trusteeship. Amongst them, one was even Jayaprakash Narayan.[1] The situation is now changing, except for those who are still committed Marxists. The primary cause of this change is the disappointing experience with both free and state capitalism. This is even having its impact in the West, where a search for a third alternative is on and some experiments are being made on lines somewhat akin to trusteeship.[2] The second cause has been the removal of all suspicions and doubts regarding Gandhiji's theory of trusteeship by his talk with Louis Fischer in 1942, his later statements, the publication in 1952 of the draft formula of trusteeship which had Gandhiji's approval, the Bhoodan movement of Vinoba applying the trusteeship idea to land, and further clarifications made by him and other eminent Sarvodaya thinkers in the post-Gandhi period.

In fact, this shift in thinking had started in India with the publication of M.L. Dantwala's *Gandhism Reconsidered* in 1944. It, however, assumed greater dimensions in the early seventies with the revaluation of Gandhiji during his birth centenary. V.K.R.V. Rao found in 1970 Gandhiji's vision of

---

Reprinted from *Gandhi Marg*, November-December 1985, pp. 577-86.

trusteeship "prophetic for the world" and, according to J.D. Sethi, "in trusteeship, Gandhi produced a grand alternative to the prevailing economic organizations whether in the communist or capitalist countries."[3] However, what we are here concerned with are the ideas of Vinoba on trusteeship and the clarification he brought to it.

Vinoba had been especially attracted to Gandhiji by the latter's speech at the opening ceremony of Banaras Hindu University in 1915, which had been attended by many Indian princes bedecked in their jewellery. He told them, much to the consternation of many. "There is no salvation for India unless you strip yourselves of the jewellery and hold it in trust for your countrymen in India."[4] This was one of the earliest utterances of Gandhiji advocating economic trusteeship, which, in common parlance, has assumed the more comprehensive name of "trusteeship", as Gandhiji's concept undoubtedly was. This theory had its basis in his ethical principles of non-stealing and non-possession. His idea of non-possession extended also to one's physical body, with all that went with it including talents. He once said: "The body does not belong to us. While it lasts, we must use it as a trust handed over to our charge."[5] This was also the message conveyed by his life. His whole self was fully dedicated to the service of humanity.

The same was true of Vinoba, who subscribed fully both theoretically and in practice to the basic theory of trusteeship, designated by Dada Dharmadhikari as the "Absolute or Permanent Theory of Trusteeship" as against the limited economic theory called by him as "Transitional Trusteeship."[6] However, our primary concern here is with this transitional trusteeship as it developed at the hands of Vinoba. To deal with it, it will be pertinent to begin with Gandhiji himself at the place he left it at the time of his death. Gandhiji's ideas on this trusteeship had gone on evolving for some twenty-five years by way of clarification to the questionings and criticisms of those who found it difficult to reconcile themselves to it. From this viewpoint, the draft formula of trusteeship referred to earlier, is important. According to it, the trusteeship idea gave no quarter to capitalism and aimed at transforming the present capitalist order into an egalitarian one. It, however, gave the present owning class an opportunity to reform itself. The idea rejected any right of private property except insofar as it was permitted by society for its own welfare. It did not exclude legislation of ownership and use of wealth and laid down that under the state-regulated ownership an individual would not be free to hold or use his wealth for his selfish satisfaction or in disregard of the interest of society. It involved both the fixing of minimum and maximum incomes, allowing only such disparity between them as might be reasonable and equitable. At the same time, these incomes were liable to revision from time to time so as to reduce this disparity, and ultimately to obliterate it altogether. Lastly, under a Gandhian economic order, trusteeship also meant that the character of production would be determined by social necessity and not by personal whim or greed.[7] Gandhiji however, did not get an opportunity to see it implemented by any industrialist or businessman, since they did not evince any enthusiasm for it and he also died in about two years. The draft itself was only published some four years after his death.

Now coming to Vinoba, we do not find him saying anything directly about trusteeship before 1945, though there are some ideas in his earlier writings which have a bearing on the subject. In one of his articles published in the weekly

Maharashtra Dharma (1924-1927), he divided the methods of livelihood into three groups, namely, *bhiksha* (alms), *vyavasaya* (business) and *chori* (theft). *Bhiksha* is that in which one gives his utmost to society and takes only the minimum required by him, and that too with a sense of obligation. In *vyavasaya*, the two are in balance, while in theft one takes more than he gives. Vinoba placed thieves and dacoits, managers and administrators, policemen and soldiers, officers and their assistants, lawyers and doctors, teachers and preachers, industrialists and businessmen in the third group.[8] As is evident, it was the first group which had his approval. Then we find him rejecting the concept of 'haves' and 'have-nots' in his *Swaraj Sastra*, first published in 1942. He argued therein that all were 'haves' and none, a 'have-not'. If the rich have money power, the so-called poor were rich in labour power.[9]

The first direct statement was in reply to some students' question about his concept of trusteeship. Vinoba told them that the word 'trusteeship' could even be used by those who were really no trustees at all, though Gandhiji used it in a good sense. There were always people in society needing protection and guidance at every step. Children were an obvious example, but there could be others as well. That was implied in trusteeship idea. However, estates could be brought under public ownership and rules framed for their management. If they were not observed, there should be some authority to remove such trustees. If the wealthy did not use their wealth for public good, they could be deprived of it. All this followed from the definition of the word 'trustee' itself. But violence had no place in this action. On being questioned if legislation did not mean violence, Vinoba said that a desirable legislation reflecting the will of the people signified nonviolence. A law passed and enforced with the help of the military would certainly come in the category of violence, but not a legislation which commands the sanction of public opinion.[10]

Vinoba clarified his ideas further in his 'Introduction' to K.G. Mashruwala's *Gandhi and Marx* (1951), and in many of his speeches during his Bhoodan-Gramdan trek. In his 'Introduction', he expressed his own lack of attraction for the term 'trusteeship', and gave another word of his own for it, namely *Vishwasta-vritti*, the attitude of confidence. He, however, did not much dilate upon this new term besides observing that social life depended upon mutual confidence. Parents reposed confidence in their children, children in their parents, and neighbours in one another. A social order based on mutual confidence meant a harmonious planning of the varied and peculiar capacities of every member of that society. This was well expressed by the Sanskrit word *loka-sangraha* (accommodation and adjustment of everyone or the total well-being of all). The use of one's capacities, he said, for the good of all from a feeling of confidence was implicit in individual non-possession.[11] That is how Vinoba linked the 'transitional' trusteeship to 'permanent' trusteeship.

Vinoba's 'Introduction' was originally in Marathi. To make clear to the English reader the meaning of *Vishwasta-vritti*, the translator gave it as an "attitude of confidence" in accordance with the sentences following it. But it seems to me that the term implies something more as well, which I shall discuss later. To continue with other ideas in the 'Introduction', Vinoba expressed his full agreement with Mashruwala's views in the book. Hence it is important to know what Mashruwala had said in it. He had referred to an important article of his, which was published by Gandhiji after his corrections in the *Harijan* weekly in 1936. Mashruwala had written in it regarding the institution of private property: "On this matter Gandhiji has perhaps more radical views than the most extreme Communist. He would like to dispossess every person of all kinds of belongings. If he tolerates the institution of private property, it is not because he loves it, or holds it to be necessary for the progress of humanity, but because he has yet to discover a truthful and nonviolent method of abolishing that institution!"[12] Another important remark of Mashruwala is that "the theory of trusteeship applies not only to tangible and transferable property, but also to places of power and position and to intangible and non-transferable property such as muscular energy of a labourer and the talents of Helen Keller."[13] This reminds one of an observation of A.E. Morgan of the TVA fame that "modern life, with its rapidly growing complexities greatly increases the number of situations in which the only sound relation is that of a trustee, and the growth of a sense of responsibility has not been sufficiently rapid to meet these changing conditions."[14]

A third remark of Mashruwala is: "Expropriation is unnecessary and unjust if the present holders consent to fulfill the obligations of trustees. An attempt be made first to convert them to that position. Compensation is unnecessary because no trustee is compensated upon removal."[15] These various ideas of his must be presumed to express also the thinking of Vinoba on trusteeship.

As regards the term *Vishwasta-vritti*, according to the Sanskrit-English Dictionary of V. S. Apte, the word *Vishwasta* has several meanings. One of them is also 'trustworthy' or 'capable of inspiring confidence'. Hence *Vishwasta-vritti* also means an attitude capable of inspiring confidence or a trustworthy attitude. I think that when Vinoba gave this word, he also implied that those who profess to be trustees, must conduct themselves in a manner as to inspire in others trust in themselves. This interpretation is justifiable on two grounds. First, there is a support for it in one of the statements of Vinoba himself. Vinoba had been fond of explaining the relationship between a trustee and the beneficiaries by using the example of a father and his sons. According to him, the attitude of the trustees must correspond to that of fathers, who take greater care of their sons than of themselves, and who try to train them to stand on their own legs and to become as capable of managing things as they are. At one place he said: "Due to differences in intelligence, physical strength, experience, etc., *Vishwasta-vritti* shall be needed at all places and at all times, including different societies and different countries, and they would be interdependent. In other words, a son will be reliable for his father and the father for his son. A householder will be reliable for a *brahmachari*, and the latter for the former. One's country will be reliable for other countries, and they reliable for it."[16] Here Vinoba talked of the reliability of one for the other, and this shows that the second meaning of *Vishwasta*, namely, capable of inspiring confidence, was also in his mind. Secondly, this meaning also explains why the term 'trusteeship' has lost its attraction, and 'distrust' has replaced 'trust'. The behaviour of the so-called trustees, in general, has not been such as to inspire confidence in others.

An analysis of Vinoba's speeches during his Bhoodan-Gramdan trek shows that he did not hold that the only motivation in society was narrow selfish interest or greed, and that in trusteeship immoral earnings could have no place, since the two were contradictory. Vinoba's concept of wealth was that it should always be flowing since it is called *dravya*, the word '*drava*' meaning something liquid. A society where people do not constantly think of others is a dead society. He laid stress not on individual property but on individual responsibility. He regarded it a mission of his life to abolish the institution of private property, and he felt that it was also the need of the age. To the charge laid against him by some who had also been near to Gandhi that he was deviating from Gandhi, who did not want to abolish private property but only wanted the rich to treat their employees better, his emphatic reply was that he too had lived with Gandhiji and he understood his ideas. Gandhiji did not want to retain ownership. He only said: "So long as there is ownership, the owners should act as trustees."[17]

Vinoba was not only opposed to accumulation by individuals but also to the collection of permanent or long-term funds for public purposes, approving their collection to meet the expenditure of any activity for a year or two only. He had objected to their funds being deposited in banks by constructive institutions, since the banks could utilise them in any manner they liked, including for purposes that were against the aims and objectives of those institutions.[18]

Vinoba was constantly exhorting people during his countrywide trek to accept the idea of trusteeship and mould their individual and social life accordingly. The various forms of *dan*, donations, initiated by him aimed at changing the mentality of all kinds of people and to facilitate their steps towards trusteeship. Besides the main land-gifts, they were *sampattidan* (donation of wealth or income), *sadhan-dana* (donation of the means of production), *buddhi-dana* (donation of one's special talents for the service of others), *Shrama-*

dana (free labour), etc. To these was later added *jeevan-dana* (dedication of one's life to the cause of Sarvodaya) by Jayaprakash Narayan to which Vinoba subscribed whole-heartedly by formally dedicating his life as well. Wherever Vinoba went he laid stress on the form of trusteeship that suited the audience. He would ask in an industrial town for the donation of industries, their socialization, their cooperatives, joint management by owners and labourers, and would ask both of them to realize their responsibilities. He would advise that a son of the owner should also work as a labourer and of the profit earned a part should be donated for public purposes, while the rest be equitably divided between the owner and the labourers. He asked businessmen for *sampattidan*, and reminded the poor that there were also people poorer than they, and that they should make some sacrifice for them.[19] All this gave a jolt to the institution of private property, though it proved only temporary.

An observation may be made here. Vinoba, while advocating complete abolition of the institution of private property, did not go into the intricacies of it. This was probably due to the nature of the audience he generally used to address, and that too in the context of a movement which aimed at becoming a people's movement. This lacuna, however, was filled in by Dada Dharmadhikari, who had been more of an intellectual. He differentiated between private property and personal property, the latter standing for things of personal use. He would allow personal property, though at the same time he would discourage an attitude of ownership towards them.[20]

So much about Vinoba's ideas on trusteeship, which were generally received with approval. However, critics were not lacking, though only a few of them were vocal. A few Gandhians like Maganbhai Desai and Harekrushna Mehtab had even charged him, as indicated earlier, of going against the wishes of Gandhiji in his plea for the abolition of private property. Vinoba's reply to that charge has already been cited. What needs to be mentioned here is that this charge had proved somewhat still-born, since all eminent Gandhian thinkers were one in lauding his movement and were ranged on his side.[21] In view of Mashruwala's 1936 article, the charge does not merit any discussion. It was not taken seriously then, and if any doubts were left at all, they were finally set at rest by the statement of Pyarelal that "Gandhiji's idea is today reborn and is being pursued with spectacular success by Vinoba Bhave. It promises to usher in the 'thorough social awakening' of which Gandhiji had prophetically talked on the 13th December, 1942, in the Detention Camp at Poona, and to become the spearhead of a nonviolent revolution whose implications reach far and wide."[22] It is a different matter altogether that the expectations raised by Vinoba's movement were not fulfilled.

There are, however, a few other observations which need consideration. Ganesh D. Gadre observed in a seminar paper of 1968: "Acharya Vinoba Bhave is striving to implement the concept of trusteeship in the agricultural sector of Indian economy.... But the major concentration of wealth and power are centered in the cities. The Bhoodan-Gramdan movement has not spelled out how its principles are to operate in trade and industry."[23] In saying this Gadre had pointed out a real weakness of the Sarvodaya movement. This weakness, I think, was also partly responsible for the failure of the Bhoodan-Gramdan movement. But it may also be urged that Bhoodan had an incidental birth and it was only after receiving a good response that Vinoba started demanding one-sixth of land from landowners. The idea of complete renunciation of ownership of land got a concrete shape still later in Gramdan. Thus the whole thing had grown slowly, step by step. As regards the city people, Vinoba had given a call for *sadhanadan* and *sampattidan* quite early in the movement. Had they also received a good response, the idea of trusteeship in business and industry, it may well be surmised, would have been given further shape and efforts made in that direction. But it did not happen, and hence this deficiency in the movement. Probably, Vinoba had also before him the fate of the trusteeship formula approved by Gandhiji and handed over to G.D. Birla.[24] Moreover, the efforts of Jayaprakash Narayan in the mid-sixties in that direction did not also bear fruit.[25] The trade unions themselves were not enthusiastic about it,[26] probably because they were more interested in larger payments than in the sharing of the responsibilities of management.

Then there is also an observation of Jayaprakash Narayan. In his Foreword to Folkerit Wilken's book, *New Forms of Ownership in Industries*, published in 1962, he wrote that "it is difficult to say what impact the publication of this book will have here. As far as the Sarvodaya movement is concerned, much depends upon Vinobaji. If he shows some warmth for the ideas put forth here, there is a fair chance that it will stimulate thought — and one hopes action — in our circle."[27] It is not clear what he really implied by saying all this. It is however possible that what he meant to convey was that if Vinoba took interest, he could influence Gandhian institutions to adopt some form of industrial democracy. Earlier in his Foreword he had mentioned that the Khadi institutions worked on a non-profit-making basis and practised more or less equality in wages, but what they lacked in was industrial democracy. If my surmise is correct, one cannot be sure that even if Vinoba had desired it, he could have brought about the change. First, his influence in the sixties was not what it had been in the fifties. The respect for him had not decreased, but his influence had. Secondly, the hold of the Gandhian values on the public mind was on the wane, and it was, I think, having some impact on the elder Gandhians as well. Thirdly, the persons heading these institutions had been having, as I understand, a genuine feeling that the institutions they had built up by their dedicated efforts during the last forty years or so, would not be very safe in the hands of the new generation of workers who lack in requisite commitment to Gandhian ideas and values. Lastly, with time, they had also learnt how to deal with Vinoba, if his advice did not suit them. However, an interesting question which arises in connection with the above remark is: Did Jayaprakash Narayan ever talk to Vinoba about it, and if he did, what was Vinoba's reaction? There is no information available about it yet.

The third and the last observation is of Kamala Gadre who characterises Vinoba's Bhoodan-Gramdan efforts for trusteeship as a 'feeble fight', while calling Rammanohar Lohia's attempt to introduce a Draft Trusteeship Bill in the House of the People in 1967 as a 'vigorous thrust' for trusteeship. She is critical of Vinoba for keeping his movement non-political.[28] This criticism of the non-political nature of the movement is not new, and has been much discussed. Hence one need not go into it here. What rather seems strange is that Vinoba's efforts which continued for more than fourteen years and in which he went on foot from village to village in all parts of the country, covering about 80,000 kms, are called 'feeble', while a mere attempt to introduce a bill is pronounced a 'vigorous thrust'. Comparisons are always odious, but one is constrained to say that Vinoba's efforts will always occupy a far higher place in the minds of objective students. As V.K.R.V. Rao says: "There is, however, no denying the fact that this great one-man campaign (of Bhoodan) did shake the country, at least for a short period and made some erosion in the concept of private property at its most sensitive point in Indian society, namely, agricultural land. To that extent, his *bhoodan* movement has been of educational value in preparing the country for a radical change in land and property relations at a later stage."[29] Admitting that the initial impulses generated have worn away, he further says: "All the same, the hard blow that Vinoba Bhave struck at the institution of private property in land by the weapon of nonviolent and moral and spiritual force is an important contribution to the concept of Indian socialism, giving it a flavour and an accent not found in Western socialist movement."[30] These two observations should suffice to show the value of Vinoba's single-minded efforts for the reconstruction of Indian society on the basis of Gandhi's trusteeship idea, which has great relevance in the world of today.

NOTES AND REFERENCES

1. In his *Why Socialism*?, written in the mid-thirties, Jayaprakash Narayan had rejected the theory of trusteeship, describing Gandhism as a compound of "timid economic analysis, good intentions and ineffective moralising". Bimal Prasad (ed.), *A Revolutionist's Quest* (Oxford University Press, Delhi, 1980), p. 41.
2. See S.D. Tripathi, "Experiments in Trusteeship Management", *Gandhi Marg*, October 1973.
3. V.K.R.V. Rao, *The Gandhian Alternative to Western Socialism* (Bharatiya Vidya Bhavan, Bombay, 1970), p. 51; J.D. Sethi, *Gandhian Values and Twentieth Century Challenges* (Publications Division, 1979), p 38. See also B.N. Ganguli, *Gandhi's Social Philosophy* (Vikas, 1972) (reprinted by National Gandhi Museum

in 2000), pp. 270-80, and J.D. Sethi, *Gandhi Today* (Vikas, 1979), Chapter 7.

4. N.K. Bose, *Studies in Gandhism* (Calcutta, 1947), p. 81.
5. M.K. Gandhi, *From Yeravda Mandir* (Ahmedabad, 1945), p. 8
6. *Sarvodaya Darshan* (Varanasi, 1957), pp. 284-87.
7. M.K. Gandhi, *Trusteeship* (Ahmedabad, I960), pp. 39-40.
8. Vinoba, *Madhukar* (Varanasi, 1962).
9. Vinoba, *Swaraj Sastra* (Bombay, 1945), p. 15.
10. Vinoba, *Kranti Darshan* (Varanasi, 1962), pp. 35-38.
11. Vinoba's Introduction to K.G. Mashruwala, *Gandhi and Marx* (Ahmedabad, 1951).
12. K.G. Mashruwala, op. cit, p. 78.
13. ibid., p. 79.
14. *The Long Road* (Navajivan, Ahmedabad, 1958), p. 75.
15. Op. cit., pp. 81-82.
16. Speech dated 20 October 1953 in Vinoba, *Bhoodan-Ganga*, Nirmala Deshpande (ed.), Vol. II (Varanasi, 1957).
17. All these ideas lie scattered in the eight volumes of Vinoba, *Bhoodan-Ganga*. Also *Bhoodan Yajna*, II-13, p. 7.
18. *Proceedings of the Rau Sarvodaya Sammelan of 1949*, p. 62. The idea also finds support in Dada Dharmadhikari, op. cit., p. 284. See also *Harijan*, 23 June 1951 and 31 May 1952.
19. Speeches dated 27 February 1958, 3 October 1956, etc. in the volumes of *Bhoodan Ganga*, edited by Nirmala Deshpande, Varanasi.
20. Dada Dharmadhikari, *Samyayoga Ki Rah Par* (Varanasi, 1956), p. 50 and Sarvodya Darshan, pp. 281-82.
21. Kaka Kalelkar in Hindi *Gandhi Marg* of January 1958, J.B. Kripalani in *Vigil* of 12 April 1952, and Dada Dharmadhikari in *Sarvodaya Darshan*, p. 287. For criticism see Maganbhai Desai in Hindi *Gandhi Marg*, March 1979, p. 29, and Harekrushna Mehtab in *Harijan*, 11 September 1955.
22. Pyarelal, *Towards New Horizons* (Ahmedabad, J959), p. 94.
23. Shankarrao Deo, *Could We Not Agree on Gandhi's Alternative to Capitalism* (Thanjavur, 1969), p. 10.
24. See Pyarelal, op. cit, for the history of the draft formula.
25. Hindi article of G.B. Deshpande in *Sarvodaya Samaj Sammelan Smarika*, 1983.
26. Kamala Gadre writes of the hesitant approach of the INTUC towards trusteeship in her book, *The Coming Struggle for Trusteeship* (Trusteeship Forum, New Delhi, 1971), pp. 65-70. She is silent on

the attitude of other unions, but I think that the same was true of them as well. G.B. Deshpande admits it in a way in his *Smarika* article mentioned above.

27. Folkert Wilken's book is a Sarva Seva Sangh Prakashan publication.
28. Kamla Gadre, op. cit., pp. 51, 53 and 55. It may be remarked here that it was not in the nature of Vinoba to do any 'fighting'. He followed the method of satyagraha, as he conceived it.
29. Op. cit., p. 75. The words in parenthesis are mine.
30. ibid., p. 76.

APPENDIX 2

Vinoba and Satyagraha

Vinoba came into public limelight when Gandhiji nominated him as the first Satyagrahi for the 'Individual Satyagraha' of 1940. Introducing him then in the *Harijan* he dilated upon his great qualities, his dedication to constructive work, his capacity to inspire others and his total opposition to war. Later, he even deemed him to be capable of writing on the science of nonviolence.[1]

However, Vinoba's ideas on the place and form of satyagraha in present-day India have come in for a great deal of criticism first from the late Ram Manohar Lohia and, later on in the seventies in the context of the Bihar Movement, from his own colleagues and fellow-workers who had earlier defended him against the attacks of Dr Lohia. Hence an attempt is being made here to trace the development of Vinoba's attitude towards satyagraha, to examine his 'deviations' from Gandhiji to explain the reasons thereof and, lastly, to discuss its consequences for the Sarvodaya movement.

DEVELOPMENT OF HIS ATTITUDE

During the lifetime of Gandhiji, Vinoba had participated in several satyagrahas, namely, the Nagpur Flag Satyagraha of

---

Reprinted from *Gandhi Marg*, October 1980, pp. 385-394.

1923, the Vykom Satyagraha of 1925, and the Individual Satyagraha already referred to. He was also arrested and imprisoned in 1932 and 1942. This gives an impression that Vinoba was in favour of satyagraha but it is belied by his book *Swaraj Sastra*, first published in Marathi in 1942.

Therein he seems to differentiate between satyagraha against state and that against society, and, in the manner of Gandhiji, lays down some stringent conditions for the former. According to him: "Though in a good state non-cooperation and resistance are occasional and depend upon time and circumstances, they occupy a permanent place in social life."[2] As regards satyagraha against state, he said that "every member of the general public must feel that law is made by the majority opinion of the people, that people can therefore change it, and if it is not opposed to morality, he should obey it voluntarily, joyfully and unreservedly, even if as an individual he does not like it. . . . It is only an individual who thus as a rule gives his cooperation that has the right, when occasion demands it, to offer non-cooperation and resistance."[3] This statement shows that Vinoba was particular about the quality of satyagrahis and, by implication, he discouraged mass satyagraha. In doing so, as we shall see later, he was very much echoing the caution of Gandhiji.

His disinclination towards the resisting type of satyagraha came into the open at the Sevagram Constructive Workers' Conference, held in March 1948 after the death of Gandhiji. On its deciding to have an association of those who subscribed to the ideas and ideals of Gandhiji the question of its name arose. The subcommittee favoured 'Satyagraha Mandal' but it was changed to 'Sarvodaya Samaj' on Vinoba's objection that the former name would arouse expectations in the people that it would be launching satyagrahas in the popular sense.[4] And soon after, he started educating the public on the wider connotation of the term. He said at a meeting: "Gandhiji taught us several things, but the most important of them is 'satyagraha'. It has a very wide connotation. Faith in truth in every conduct of life is satyagraha. In this sense even prayer is satyagraha. Restraint in action, thought and speech is satyagraha. The practice of rising early in the morning is satyagraha. However, in a very restricted sense it also means 'a method of resisting injustice'. The people are familiar with this meaning only."[5] Speaking on that very occasion on fasts, he said: "Fast has a special place among the spiritual weapons of nonviolence, but it is being misused today either as pressure tactics or to draw attention towards some grievance. It is not proper to use this mighty weapon for petty purposes."[6] He advised its use only as a last resort by a person who possessed a pure mind and discernment, was free from passions, hatred and egoism, and had a long record of public service, provided the situation warranted it. Except in the purest of persons, the inner voice might prove to be the voice of Satan.[7] He repeated these ideas when fasts were undertaken for linguistic states in 1953.

The topic of satyagraha was often cropping up during his Bhoodan-tour, and Vinoba always stressed that "it was a way of living, a way of doing and, in particular situations, a way of remedying".[8] The test he laid down for a conflict resolution satyagraha was that it should disarm the opponent. In his words, "When the sun rises, darkness is dispelled. True satyagraha has similar power. The very sight of it compels a man to think where he has been unwilling to think, and to purify his thinking when his thoughts have run on very different lines. The veils of illusion are removed and there is a new openness in his mind."[9] It should assist in right thinking.[10] Vinoba is of the view that truth itself should be allowed to do its work, and instead of insistence on one's truth, there should be receptivity to the truth on the other side.[11]

But he did not rule out non-cooperation and resistance altogether. In 1952 when some leading politicians argued against them in a democracy, he explained his ideas at some length and concluded by saying that "if a democratic government does a grave injustice and the hearts of the persons at the helm do not melt while righteous men feel that a grave injustice is being done, satyagraha may become necessary; and I say no one can rule out such satyagraha."[12] Here, however, he seems to be thinking in terms of individual satyagraha rather than a corporate one.

Vinoba looked upon his Bhoodan tour as a form of satyagraha.[13] He once said in 1958: "In a democracy, satyagraha can never take the form of exercise of pressure. Its correct form is that of the change of heart. The pressure form can go well with other politics. In a democracy the form will be either of the change or of entry into the heart through constructive work."[14] Earlier that year, he had laid down four principles of satyagraha, namely, (i) satyagraha is not negative but positive, (ii) it should proceed from gentle to gentler and to the gentlest, (iii) one should feel happy on hearing the very word 'satyagraha', and (iv) let there be no insistence on one's part leaving it for the truth itself to do so.[15] To these ideas Vinoba has stuck to this day. There was a crisis in the Sarvodaya movement on the issue of support to and participation in the Bihar Movement when a vast majority of Sarvodaya workers wanted to do so under the leadership of Jayprakash Narayan. Even then Vinoba did not change his stand, but to avoid a split he agreed to a compromise allowing individual Sarvodayites to participate in it provided the three conditions of adherence to truth, nonviolence and self-restraint were observed. It was also hoped that the movement for the dissolution of State legislatures would not be extended elsewhere. The movement was treated as an experiment to be allowed with some necessary precautions.[16]

Despite such a theoretical position, Vinoba had permitted some Satyagrahis and he himself went twice on fast. In 1962 he permitted workers in Tamilnadu to start satyagraha against the eviction of tenants, and again in 1965 on the question of Meenakshi Temple land. It was under his advice that in i960 a campaign was launched by workers against indecent film posters. He also did not stand in the way of Harivallabh Parikh of Gujarat who resorted to satyagraha against the illegal demands of the feudal lords, eviction of tenants, corruption of the police and high-handedness of the officials in a tribal area. He was also not averse to it to compel the Rajasthan State Government to declare prohibition in that State. And, above all, he himself went on a fast in 1965 when there were riots in Tamilnadu against the adoption of Hindi as the national language by the Central Government, and again in 1979, over the question of cow-slaughter ban in Kerala and West Bengal. Only recently he has advised workers to prevent cows and bullocks being taken for slaughter to these two states.

However, in all these cases of satyagraha the issues were definite and limited, and they neither involved large areas, nor a very large number of people. As already indicated, he has not been against individual satyagraha for valid reasons, and it also seems that he does not disfavour group satyagrahas in matters which despite the sanction of law and public opinion, are not being implemented. Whatever his general attitude, in particular cases he has decided taking into consideration the issues involved and the quality of the persons undertaking the satyagraha.

'DEVIATIONS' FROM GANDHIJI

The charge of deviation from Gandhiji against Vinoba had been most vehemently put forward by Dr Lohia, who even went to the length of saying that he was killing Gandhiji. He found fault with him for for getting that one of the functions of satyagraha was to remove the weaknesses of the people and for failing to understand the other aspect of the teaching of Gandhiji besides that of love, which was to fight poverty, dishonesty and tyranny.[17]

Before taking up this charge, certain observations have to be made, The first relate to the difficulty of interpreting Gandhiji. It was due to this that K.G. Mashruwala, a close associate and a recognized interpreter of Gandhiji, wrote in 1952: "If there was anything like Gandhism, it died with Gandhiji. For Gandhiji alone could have the whole of it. Every one else might have something in common with him, or with everything of his plus something else of his own, but none the whole and nothing that the whole of Gandhiji. So let no associate, howsoever close, say that he is a follower, or interpreter of Gandhiji or Gandhism."[18] And this is endorsed by Jayaprakash Narayan who wrote, "One of the foremost difficult things to define is what is truly Gandhism."[19] Gandhiji also practically lived and worked prior to Indian independence, his attitude was of one step being enough for him, his actions and advice, though in consonance, with his fundamental principles of truth and nonviolence, took into consideration the circumstances of the situation as well, and it is not difficult to cite him in support of diverse views, Moreover, he never claimed to have developed the science of satyagraha in its entirety. Hence any discussion of this charge must involve some speculation.

Secondly, Gandhiji himself had advised that if there was any real inconsistency between his various statements, one would do well to take the meaning his last statement yielded unless, of course, he preferred the old.[20] Vinoba has repeated this statement of Gandhiji several times showing his preference for his latest observations.

Thirdly, Vinoba has never claimed to be a representative of Gandhiji. He only says that Gandhiji has influenced him most and that he feels that whatever he has been doing has been inspired by him and has his blessings. He once wrote: "Some have begun to look upon me as the representative of Gandhiji's ideas. . . . But there can be no bigger mistake than this. It is true that so far my life has been spent in carrying out those programmes of Gandhiji which appealed to me. But this proviso of 'which appealed to me' was always there. I gained fully from his association and ideas, and accepted whatever seemed correct to me. I left out others. Hence I am a man of my ideas."[21] He is of the view that Gandhiji has given us a line of thinking and we have to proceed further independently. To limit Gandhiji to his words and actions would be doing an injustice to him.[22] Hallam Tennyson rightly wrote about him, "Like a candle lit at a neighbouring flame, he now burns with a steady and separate light."[23]

Having made these observations, if we examine the writings of Gandhiji to discover his ideas relating to the form of satyagraha under a democracy, we find some lack of consistency. He had said before the Hunter Commission, "I can conceive the necessity of Satyagraha in opposition to the would-be full responsible self-government."[24] Again in 1930, "My nonviolence would not prevent me from fighting my countrymen on the many questions which must arise when India has become free."[25] Further, he interpreted Christ's teaching of 'resist not evil' to mean 'resist not evil with evil'.[26] All these statements provide support to the view that he did not rule out non-cooperation and civil disobedience in a democracy.

But, as against these, statements can also be cited to show his hesitation in recommending them under a democratic system. He said in 1920: "Most people do not understand the complicated machinery of government. They do not realize that every citizen silently but nonetheless certainly sustains the government of the day in ways of which he has no knowledge. Every citizen, therefore, renders himself responsible for every act of his government. And it is quite proper to support it as long as the actions of the government are bearable. But when they hurt him and his nation, it becomes his duty to withdraw his support."[27] And again in 1939: "A born democrat is a born disciplinarian. Democracy comes naturally to him who is habituated normally to yield willing obedience to all laws, human or divine. . . . Let those who are ambitious to serve democracy qualify themselves by satisfying this acid test of democracy."[28] Lastly, he said in 1946, that "total nonviolent non-cooperation has no place in popular Raj, whatever its level may be."[29] Gandhiji as interpreted by K.G. Mashruwala, would not sanction satyagraha against a popular democratic government.[30] Thus there is enough material in Gandhiji to warrant Vinoba's attitude and his search for a positive, constructive satyagraha suited to the Indian conditions today.

There are two other points as well to which attention may be drawn in this context. One relates to a consideration which Gandhiji wanted to be kept in mind by those who wished to launch a satyagraha. He said: "Satyagraha offered on every occasion reasonable or otherwise would be corrupted into *duragraha*. And if anyone takes to satya-graha without having measured his own strength and afterwards sustains defeat, he not only disgraces himself but he also brings the matchless weapon of satyagraha into disrepute by his folly."[31] It has equally been a consideration with Vinoba.[32]

The second point is that in the last analysis the doctrine of satyagraha rests upon a religious and metaphysical belief or recognition of the soul, as apart from the body, and its permanent and superior nature. And this recognition must be a living faith and not a mere intellectual grasp.[33] Gandhiji had this faith and so has Vinoba. It is this which inspires him to advocate the principle of "from gentle to gentler and to the gentlest".

It is obvious from the above that Lohia's vehement denunciation of Vinoba has no justification. Yet, it is also evident that Vinoba's emphasis is not on those forms of Satyagraha that had gained popularity in the pre-independence period. Though it would be incorrect to say that they lacked positive content, their forms certainly were largely negative, and that is probably why Gandhiji had to lay repeated emphasis on the importance of constructive work and its superiority over satyagraha. He once said, "If you make a real success of the constructive programme, you will win Swaraj for India without civil disobedience."[34]

CAUSES OF VINOBA'S ATTITUDE

It needs to be examined at some length what factors led Vinoba to disapprove of the aggressive forms of satyagraha.[35] The foremost place among them must be assigned to his mental make-up. He has primarily been a constructive worker and has a constructive frame of mind, not that of an agitator. His participation in various satyagrahas does not seem to have been born of any inner desire. In the Nagpur Flag Satyagraha he did so because he had been requested to lead it after some time, and in the other two it was at the behest of Gandhiji. He did not participate in the Salt Satyagraha but he had been arrested in 1932 for addressing a public meeting when the Congress had been declared illegal. The meeting had been arranged prior to it and hence Vinoba insisted on attending it.[36]

The second important reason is the misuse of this weapon in the post-independence period. Joan V. Bondurant writes, "A review of the contemporary history of political events in India suggests that *duragraha* and demonstration, strike and fasting — under the name of satyagraha — are the techniques of the day.[37] They seemed to justify the fears of many who had opposed Gandhiji's satyagraha during his life-time on the ground that they were bound to inculcate in the people a spirit and habit of indiscipline and anarchy.

Thirdly, Vinoba is convinced that in the democratic political set-up of the country, when people are free to propagate their ideas and to change the government they dislike, it is a mistake to adopt the negative tactics of confrontation. The internal reconstruction of the country requires the cooperation of all. No class of Indian people can be asked to quit India as the Britishers were told to do.[38] What is needed, then is to adopt methods which would help in a change of head and heart. Hence they should be assisted in right thinking and the better side of their nature should be helped to assert itself.

Moreover, Vinoba has been of the view that Sarvodaya ideas and ideals have not gained in society acceptance to the extent that Sarvodaya workers can launch any effective movement of confrontation on the basis of their own strength. This reading of Vinoba seems to have been justified by the experience of the Bihar Movement which ultimately had to rely on the support of the opposition parties, who exploited it for their own purpose and on coming to power forgot the cause of the Total Revolution.

Lastly, Vinoba considers it essential to search for a form of satyagraha which would prove effective in this age of high technological development. He says, "The new technological era has made the world smaller. Our nonviolence in this context must be powerful enough to meet the challenge of atomic weapons and to spread the message of peace. We cannot afford to waste the power of nonviolence over minor day-to-day internal struggles. Our nation must accumulate it for higher moral progress."[39] He is confident that such a form of satyagraha can be discovered, and that it does not involve any mysticism.[40]

EFFECT ON SARVODAYA MOVEMENT

To discuss the consequences of Vinoba's attitude towards non-cooperation and civil disobedience as regards the Sarvodaya movement, it would be more pertinent to examine the views of those who have been mostly in agreement with Vinoba. In a booklet published in 1971, Vasant Nargolkar, while admitting the achievements of the Bhoodan movement, says that the movement failed to fulfill the expectations it had originally aroused. It failed to solve the land problem, to have any impact on the social, economic and political situation in India, to influence the thinking of the intelligentsia, to create even a substantial following among the village masses, and to prevent communal and other disturbances through its Shanti Sena. He attributes this failure to the "rejection of satyagraha as a means of bringing about a nonviolent revolution." He says that for lack of it there has been no enthusiastic participation of the people and no involvement of the people in *gramdan* villages in the difficult task of promoting Sarvodaya ideals. Nargolkar is not opposed to Vinoba's technique, but he would like to supplement it by direct nonviolent action.[41]

What Nargolkar says finds echo in many, and much can be said for it. It may be argued that people have a psychology of theirs which needs to be considered if their cooperation is desired. Provision of some dynamic outlet for the energies of the people would have led to greater public participation, and, indirectly, to a greater control over the policies and actions of those who were in power. Since Sarvodaya had rejected parliamentary programme, it was all the more necessary for it to retain this weapon. Vinoba's ideas, though theoretically correct once the premises of Gandhian thought are accepted, lacked perception of the realities of the situation.

However, to attribute the non-achievements of the Sarvodaya movement solely to Vinoba's neglect of the weapon of nonviolent resistance would be too simplistic an explanation. It would be pertinent to observe here that the satyagrahas launched by Lohia's socialist party had neither enhanced its prestige nor its influence over the Indian masses. Moreover, the movement of Jayaprakash Narayan too failed to advance the country towards his objective.[42] Hence it is difficult to say that Vinoba's reading of the objective situation and his discouragement of the general use of nonviolent resistance did harm to the Sarvodaya movement. On the other hand, Vinoba's technique of silent, constructive work had enhanced the prestige and influence of its leaders and the one cause of the popular support that Jayaprakash Narayan's movement received was his long association with it.

Yet, when all this has been said, a feeling persists that it would have been better if satyagraha in the form of nonviolent resistance had found a greater scope in the Sarvodaya movement. But it would be unfair to blame Vinoba for that. Gandhiji is a rare phenomenon. None in the Sarvodaya movement or outside has yet been able to discover the form of nonviolent resistance suiting the realities of present-day India. On the other hand, the concept of gentle and gentler satyagraha is a great contribution of Vinoba, and it would do good both to India and the world if extensive experiments in it are also undertaken.

NOTES AND REFERENCES

1. *Harijan*, October 16, 1940 and March 3, 1946.
2. *Swaraj Sastra* (Bombay, 1945), p. 47.
3. ibid., pp. 45-46.
4. Hindi Proceedings of the Conference, pp. 59, 67-68 and Resolution No. 2 in the Appendix.
5. *Harijan Sevak*, October 17, 1948.
6. ibid.
7. ibid
8. *Vinoba Chintan*, No. 34-35, p. 507.
9. Vinoba, *Democratic Values* (Kashi, September 1962), p. 156.

10. Hindi Proceedings of Arambagh Sangh Session, pp. 25-26.
11. *Vinoba Chintan*, No. 34-35, p. 491.
12. *Harijan*, September 20, 1952.
13. *Harijan*, April 6, 1955.
14. *Vinoba Pravachan*, March 14, 1958.
15. *Bhoodan Yajna*, February 7, 1958.
    Two examples of gentle satyagraha make Vinoba's conception clearer. He once advised workers not to go on strike for better payments but to accept one rupee less in their wages as a protest measure, and thus to draw the attention of the authorities and the public to their grievances. At the same time, the path of negotiation and arbitration was to be kept open. (*Bhoodan*, 27 August 1960). The second is that of the advice he gave to a person who sought it on his satyagraha in a village for Harijans being allowed to draw water from the village well. The villagers opposed to it had offered to dig a separate well for the Harijans, and the person had asked Vinoba if he should accept their offer. Referring to it, Vinoba said, "I intend writing to him to accept the proposal.... Whatever is done presuming the existence of caste differences will only serve to strengthen those differences. At the new well the Harijans will draw water, and others as well. This will lead to unification, obliterate the differences and by and by feelings of love will develop." He further added, "Mine will be considered a weak advice in terms of the mentality of today. But it is no weak advice. It is rather a strong Bhoodan Yajna advice" (*Bhoodan Yajna* July 4, 1958).
    Vinoba's advice to Jayaprakash Narayan in 1975 to imitate Lord Krishna and to withdraw his movement would also fall under the above category.
16. Prabhas Joshi, "How Vinoba saved the Sarvodaya Movement," (*Everyman's Weekly*, July 27, 1974).
17. Onkar Sharad, *Lohia Ke Vichar* (Allahabad, 1979), p. 239.
18. *Harijan*, June 28, 1952.
19. Foreword to J. D. Sethi, *Gandhi Today* (New Delhi, 1979).
20. *Harijan*, September 30, 1939,
21. *Sarvodaya* (Hindi), August 1949, p. 7.
22. *Vinoba Pravachan* (No. 388).
23. P.D. Tandon (ed.), *Vinoba Bhave: The Man and His Mission* (Bombay), p. 98.
24. M.K. Gandhi, *Satyagraha* (Ahmedabad, 1951), p. 33.

25. Cited in G.N. Dhawan, *The Political Philosophy of Mahatma Gandhi* (Ahmedabad, 1951), p. 33.
26. Raghavan N. Iyer, *The Moral and Political Thought of Mahatma Gandhi* (Delhi, 1973), p. 274.
27. ibid., pp. 320-321.
28. *Collected Works*, Vol. LXIX, p. 43.
29. *Harijan*, July 14, 1946.
30. *Gandhi Vichar Dohan* (Ahmedabad, 1968), p. 66.
31. M.K. Gandhi, *Satyagraha in South Africa* (Ahmedabad, 1950), p. 206.
32. *Vinoba Chintan*, March 1966, p. 36.
33. Raghavan Iyer, op. cit., pp. 290-291.
34. Cited in Pyarelal, *The Last Phase*, Vol. I, p. 44.
35. R.R. Diwakar has divided the social weapon of satyagraha in three categories of constructive satyagraha, purifactory satyagraha and aggressive satyagraha in his book *Satyagraha: Its Technique and History* (Bombay, 1946), p. 47.
36. Shriman Narayan, *Vinoba: His Life and Mission* (Bombay, 1970), p. 66 and Kanti Shah, *Vinoba—Jivan Aur Karya* (Varanasi, Dec. 1979), p. 39.
37. *Conquest of Violence* (Oxford University Press, 1959), p. 44.
38. *Sarvodaya*, June 1956, p. 419,
39. *Bhoodan*, February 18, 1959.
40. *Bhoodan Yajna*, July 4, 1958 and *Sarvodaya* (Hindi), June 1955, p. 411.
41. *Nonviolent Revolution Through Satyagraha Alone* (Kainad, May 1971).
42. It is a matter of some significance that in a book carrying a Foreword from Jayaprakash Narayan, S.N. Ghosh writes: "Is JP-esque mass movement the method for such a goal? Perhaps the only cause that could save men and society are lost causes." (*The Crusade and End of Indira Raj*, New Delhi, 1978, p. 255. JP, however, makes it clear in the Foreword that "His conclusions are his own and I do not want to comment on them."

APPENDIX 3

The Bhoodan-Gramdan Movement (1951-74) – A Review

The father of the Bhoodan-Gramdan movement passed away on 15 November 1982. The movement had brought Vinoba to the international scene and now it is time to take stock of the movement initiated by him and conducted under his guidance till 1974 when the movement, as such, practically petered out, to be followed by severe differences in the Sarvodaya movement. Hence this article strictly confines itself up to that time.

HISTORY OF THE MOVEMENT

It was on 18 April 1951 that Vinoba received his first land gift in Telangana (now a part of Andhra Pradesh) when he was on a peace trek in that disturbed region. This incident, neither planned nor imagined, was a pleasant surprise to Vinoba and made him think that therein lay the potentiality of solving the land problem of India. Thus originated the Bhoodan (land gift) movement which later developed into a village gift or Gramdan movement and they together came to be collectively called the Bhoodan-Gramdan movement.

Reprinted from *Gandhi Marg*, November-December 1983, pp. 492-500.

This movement, as Vinoba repeatedly said, was not a mere movement for an equitable distribution of land. It was also a wedge for the establishment of a Sarvodaya society. Thus it was a part of a comprehensive movement, albeit a predominant part of it.

The advent of independence brought new opportunities and responsibilities and the constructive workers were not clear about their role in the altered circumstances. The two questions facing them were whether they should participate in politics and what should be the nature of their constructive activities in the changed situation. Gandhiji had answered the first question in November 1947 when he advised them to keep away from politics and to banish the very idea of the capture of power from their mind,[1] and when in his Last Will and Testament he asked the Congress to convert itself into a Lok Sevak Sangh. To deliberate on the second question, Gandhiji had called a conference of constructive workers at Sevagram in February 1948. But, a day before his departure for that place, he fell to the assassin's bullets.

The conference was held later in March and it requested Vinoba to guide the constructive workers. Thus came into existence the Sarvodaya Samaj, a loose brotherhood of those who subscribed to the ideas and ideals of Gandhiji, providing also a vogue to the term 'Sarvodaya' as a word standing for Gandhian ideas and activities.

The problem of defining the nature of constructive work was not an easy one, and it took some time for Vinoba to discover the land-gift activity around which all Sarvodaya activities could be woven and given the form of a movement for the reconstruction of man and society. Once discovered, he grasped it and, despite all the vicissitudes of the movement, his faith in it never faltered and he did not allow himself to be deflected from tackling the basic problem of land which affected the life of some thirty per cent of the population in the countryside constituting the agricultural landless labour class. He trekked the length and breadth of the country for it for some 4,500 days, covering some 75,000 kilometers.

The movement passed through several stages in regard to both momentum and allied programmes. It began as an individual activity of Vinoba, but its success first in Telangana where he secured 12,000 acres of land in fifty days, and then in the communist-free regions that lay between Wardha and Delhi when the gift averaged about 300 acres per day, infused a sense of confidence in Vinoba as well as in the Gandhian workers associated with it, and also in those who were watching its progress. This led Vinoba to demand on Gandhiji's birthday in 1951, fifty million acres of land for the landless from the whole country by 1957, and this induced the workers, first of Uttar Pradesh and later of other States, to concentrate their energy on acquiring them. Thus a personal activity assumed the form of a movement, reminding the people of the political movements of Gandhiji. This was rather a very remarkable achievement for a constructive work movement. This enthusiasm lasted till 1957 and thereafter it began to wane.

Meanwhile the movement had been transformed from a land-gift to a village-gift or Gramdan movement, in which the whole or a major part of a village was to be donated by not less than seventy-five per cent of the villagers who were required to relinquish their right of ownership over their lands in favour of the village, with power to equitably redistribute the total land among its families with a proviso for revision after some intervals. The programme of land-gifts was still there but henceforth became almost a neglected activity.

The Gramdan idea did not prove popular in the non-tribal areas and this partly accounted for the decline of the movement at the end of the 1950s. However, there was again a spurt in 1961 when Vinoba started the Bigha-Kattha campaign in Bihar demanding one-twentieth of their cultivable land from the holders, but it could be conducted for a few months only. However, its success was encouraging and led to the birth of the 'New Gramdan' idea, later called Sulabh (Easy) Gramdan.

In this Gramdan the terms had been made palatable. The landholders were required to relinquish their ownership in favour of the village on the guarantee that the land to be actually taken away from them would only be one-twentieth of their land. However, the formation of Gram Sabha and of the village chest from contribution in the form of money or labour were made a must under it.

The Sulabh Gramdan movement was specially conducted in Bihar under the personal guidance of Vinoba from 1965 to 1969. In terms of statistics much was achieved in regard to commitment to the Gramdan idea, but it was on paper only. Nevertheless, a new life was perceptible. After the Rajgir Sarvodaya Sammelan of 1969, Vinoba in his 75th year retired to his Paunar Ashram, leaving a band of a few trusted workers to complete the process of Gramdan in a few selected areas and thereby to lay the foundation for Gram Swaraj or village self-government there. In other States too, similar work was undertaken. But the efforts did not succeed and they were ultimately given up early in 1974 on the advice of Vinoba himself.

In this context, the reactions of the two leading lights who guided the intensive work in two areas of Bihar, are highly significant. Jayaprakash Narayan wrote in 1970: "As is apparent, our progress has been rather slow. In many respects, this is a difficult area. Yet we could have moved faster had the earlier stage of obtaining Gramdan pledges been properly gone through. So far we have not come across a single village where we have found the two requirements of 75 per cent of the population and 51 per cent of the land to have been fulfilled."[2] This was said some three years before the work was given up. The whole experience had produced a sense of frustration in the workers, including Jayaprakash Narayan who began doubting the correctness of the whole technique in exclusively relying on the landowning haves with little scope of initiative by the landless have-nots.

The other leading light, Dhirendra Mazumdar, while admitting failure said: "People would ask what were the results of Saharsa (the area of his work) and what happened there. Nothing as such was achieved there which could be described or shown to those who ask such questions or desire to see some tangible results. A basic revolution, which we term 'total revolution' and which we hope would lead to a completely new transformation, is not realized in a short span of time. . . . What is needed at present is to give up activity there and to allow time to the seed to grow."[3] He praised Vinoba for sensing this need and advising the workers to give up the campaign there.[4]

No matter what the explanation, the whole experience led Jayaprakash Narayan to think of other programmes for realizing his dream of a 'total revolution' by mobilizing the youths of the country in its cause, leading ultimately to a split, already referred to, in the Sarvodaya movement.

ALLIED ACTIVITIES

So much about the history of the movement proper till 1974 from the viewpoint of its ups and downs. But there is another aspect as well and it relates to allied programmes unfolded from time to time. There had been a view that Vinoba gave so many programmes that the whole movement outstripped the capacity of the workers and they even failed to achieve what they could have. However, all these programmes like *Sampattidan* (wealth-gift), *Shramdan* (labour-gift), and *Jeevandan* (life-gift) were directly related to the main movement, and others like *Shanti Sena* (Peace Army), *Sarvodaya Patra*, awakening of the women dealt with important problems which needed tackling. Moreover, they also had to be spelled out because the supporters of Sarvodaya included all kinds of persons and they needed programmes suited to them if their energies were to be harnessed for Sarvodaya. As a thinker too, it was incumbent upon Vinoba to present a far more complete view of Sarvodaya than could be conveyed by a part programme, no matter however important. After all, as indicated earlier, he aimed at a far more comprehensive revolution than a mere change in land relationship.[5]

Coming to the directly allied programmes, the movement required other gifts as well for its success. To provide means of cultivation to the poor donees of Bhoodan lands, Vinoba asked the urban rich to donate implements, bullocks and inputs and to get wells dug. This was a demand for *Sadhandan* or the gift of means. In Bihar, where he needed a vast army of workers to attain the target of 32 lakh acres, he applied for *Sampattidan* for the maintenance of workers. The demand of this gift was important in another way as well. The Bhoodan movement was an application of the principle of trusteeship, and it would have been neither wise nor fair to confine its application to land only. If Vinoba had not asked for it earlier or started any movement for it, it was due to strategic reasons.[6] Then there was also demand for *Shramdan* and *Jeevandan*, as stated earlier.

A matter which needs to be specially touched upon in the context of this movement is the use of resisting Satyagraha in it. There is no doubt about Vinoba's aversion to such Satyagrahas.[7] Yet, there had been a few occasions in the movement when he permitted them against ejectments from lands. More prominent of such instances were the Satyagraha against the eviction of tenants in Tamilnadu in 1962 and again in 1965 on the question of Meenakshi Temple land.

ACHIEVEMENTS AND FAILURES

Before actually discussing the achievements and failures of the movement, a few preliminary observations must be made. India is a big country and in terms of human power, the few thousand workers available to the movement were too few in number to prove effective. The leaders were aware of this weakness and Vinoba repeatedly told the workers that they were to act as a catalyst force in society. But such a role required exemplary qualities which these workers did not have in ample measures, primarily because of the adverse social climate prevailing in the country after independence. Secondly, the task of societal change and reconstruction was far more difficult than that of achieving independence. It became still more difficult since it had been initiated by persons, comparatively unknown and untried. Lastly, the work involved both material and attitudinal changes, and in this task the movement had to struggle against the increasing trend towards capitalistic and narrow individualistic values in society.

Under these circumstances, the achievements of the movement cannot but be deemed remarkable. I first take up its material achievements. True, it failed to attain the target of 50 million acres of land it had resolved to collect by 1957. All it could obtain was 41,94,270 acres, while the land actually distributed, according to 1975 statistics, was 12,85,738 acres. 18,57,398 were found unfit for distribution.[8] About the remaining 10,51,134 acres, my surmise is that much of it might be deserving to be written off altogether. Thus the actual achievement came only to about 3 per cent of the target, and the movement, therefore, must be pronounced as a failure. But if it is also taken into account that it was all a result of voluntary efforts and that some important political leaders, who should have cooperated, denounced it and that the government's sympathy was more verbal than real, even this success acquires significance. As Vinoba said in 1961: "The little achievement we have made so far is not at all negligible. It is, in fact inspiring. Till today no political party or organisation of the country has been able to distribute one million acres, nay not even half as much land to the poor. The Congress swears by the landless labourers and the P.S.P., the Communist Party and the Jana Singh all are for giving land to the tillers. The Government also promises to provide landless with land. But the combined distribution of all these agencies also is not to the extent of one million acres."[9]

In this context it must also be mentioned that K.R. Nanekar and S.V. Khandewale, who made a study of land gifts in Vidarbha,[10] found some disparity between the official figures of the Bhoodan Mandal and the initial donations. The former figures were 1,09,999.27 acres while the initial donations were found to be of 94,427.71 acres. The difference is thus of 15 per cent. While this warns us against the total correctness of the figures given out by the Sarva Seva Singh office, it does not belie Vinoba's above observation.

Coming to the Gramdans, the figure of 1,68,058 villages[11] is quite impressive, but, for the most part, they were merely paper commitments, and that too generally without an understanding of its implications. However, they did signify some readiness on the part of a considerable number of people to relinquish their absolute right of ownership over their lands in favour of the village, and the government, had it the requisite political will, could have utilized the social climate generated by the movement to limit that right.

Of the other gifts, statistics are available of Sampattidan only. Though it was never launched as a movement, Vinoba had been repeatedly appealing to the moneyed class to donate a part of their income, preferably one-sixth, for such specified Sarvodaya purposes as maintenance of workers, providing means of cultivation to the Bhoodan donees, spread of Sarvodaya ideas, etc. But the response was poor for various reasons which we need not go into here. Between 1952 and 1963, the total amount received in Sampattidan had come to about 3.25 lakh rupees, the highest in a single year being 61 thousand rupees.[12] This indicates that the movement had no worthwhile impact on the city people, and therein lay its very great weakness.

With regard to rehabilitation and reconstruction work in large Bhoodan tracts and in villages donated under the old Gramdan, the general policy was not to involve the movement in it. Vinoba had once said: "I am not really worried about how the work of reconstruction will proceed in the Gramdan villages. The task of building up a new society of the Free and Equal in the Gramdan villages is a responsibility which all have to share. It is not our private or personal commitment. I am out to pose problems, not to solve them. I am not a full-stop; I am a question mark. Creating a climate of opinion wherein people voluntarily give up their private ownership is my task."[13] The probable reasons for this attitude were two. First, had this work also been taken up, a task already stupendous would have become still more so. Secondly, there was a dearth of workers in general and of such in particular who possessed the necessary expertise for such a task. It had also been felt that the Sarva Seva Singh devoted to the task of education in the widest sense was not fit to shoulder executive tasks.[14] In the Koraput Gramdan area in Orissa where the work had been taken up on an experimental basis, the experience had not been encouraging. However, some workers and organizations did take it up. A few outstanding examples for which some information is available are those of Rangpur (Gujarat), Govindpur (Uttar Pradesh), and Barachatti (Bihar). In these tribal areas where the work is still continuing, some Western organisations have been giving financial aid. In some other Gramdan areas also, as those of Tamil Nadu, changes for the better had been reported, though the development followed no uniform pattern.[15]

Such had been, in brief, the material achievements and failures of the movement. As regards attitudinal transformation, the propagation of ideas combined with the above material achievements, could not but affect the mind of the thinking people. The movement directly influenced the life of the workers and through them of many more. By adapting Gandhiji's ideas to the solution of a basic problem, the movement kept his ideas of social reconstruction more than alive at a period when the tendency of the educated was to reject them as irrelevant. It kindled interest in the individuals to study the ideas of Gandhiji and to reassess their relevance.

The movement struck at the very concept of the right of private property at a time when no political party, including the Communist Party, dared to do so and when it had been sanctified in the Constitution. There was even a period in the movement in Bihar when land had ceased to be a marketable commodity. It created a social climate for the curbing of selfish propensities in the interest of the good of the society, for the uplift of the weakest sections of society and for the establishment of social and economic justice. Agrarian legislations of the post-independence period had certainly abolished the intermediaries, but the dread of uneconomic holdings had prevented the governments from doing justice to the landless agricultural labour.[16] The movement focused the attention of all on the plight of that class, and since then every government has been professing to do something for them.

Attitudinal changes are not easy to measure, but the value of thought propagation, a very important aspect of the movement, cannot be denied, and it is beyond doubt that by taking Gandhian ideas to every nook and corner of the country, the movement had initiated a process of attitudinal change which under propitious conditions could have crystallized.

WEAKNESSES OF THE MOVEMENT

It is also necessary to examine the weaknesses of the movement in the form of the mistakes committed and external difficulties encountered. It is easier to do it today with hindsight. The leaders themselves had realized some mistakes of the strategy in the light of the principle of nonviolence itself in the course of the movement and had tried to rectify them. They related to dependence of the movement on permanent funds, too much reliance on the mechanism of organization,[17] lack of faith in the land donors to distribute themselves the lands to the deserving landless, etc. However, it appears that some mistakes persisted till the end.

The first major mistake was to concentrate energy on Gramdan to the neglect of Bhoodan. The Gramdan idea, howsoever commendable, was utopian if we consider the strength and caliber of the workers. The Bhoodan had brought some tangible benefits to the landless and the movement should not have allowed it to suffer by neglect.

The second mistake was to concentrate even in Gramdan on securing extensive commitment to the idea and to go on postponing intensive work in select areas, which would have presented a Sarvodaya model of development. Emphasis on this work in recent years was an acknowledgment of that mistake.

The third mistake, and a very serious one from ideological viewpoint was to allow the lure of the fulfillment of the targets to dominate the movement to such an extent that the very principle of acquiring land or village gifts by explaining to the people the fundamental ideas underlying them, came to be mostly violated. Had it been adhered to, the achievements in terms of figures might have been less but some changes must have taken place in social values.

The fourth mistake relates to the failure in devising some

short-term strategy for the solution of the pressing problems of the people and for influencing the policies of the government. Because of it, the movement increasingly lost touch with the people.

In addition to these mistakes — and there may be a few others as well there was a basic external difficulty too which the movement had faced all along. Its method involved the cooperation of all, but it failed to evoke it. The attitude of the intellectuals with some exceptions was either of indifference or of opposition. Most of the English periodicals, which played a greater role in influencing those who mattered and in the formation of educated opinion, neglected the movement as if it was of no consequence. The Marxian intellectuals with their sympathy for the poor and the exploited were expected to show greater understanding of the movement, but they had their own obsession. Though they commended the objective of the movement, they rejected the method adopted and they declared that the class struggle was the only way.

The movement demanded a social dynamism, which was constantly being undermined both by the government and by the political parties. The welfareism of the governments with all its concomitants discouraged public voluntary efforts, while the opposition parties did the same by laying all blame on the party in power and by promising to set every thing right if voted to power. The life that the movement had showed in early years was greatly due to the fact that it took some time for the social dynamism of the pre-Independence period to wither away. However, this does not mean that further probe into the weaknesses is not required. It would only prove beneficial, providing guidance to those who are wedded to nonviolence.

To conclude, taking an overall view, it cannot be gainsaid that this movement as led and guided by Vinoba, despite all its real and apparent shortcomings, would ever be deemed as a glorious attempt for a peaceful nonviolent solution of a basic problem of Indian society and through it for a nonviolent reconstruction of that society.

NOTES AND REFERENCES

1. D.G. Tendulkar, *Mahatma* (Popular Prakashan, Bombay, 1954), Vol. VIII, pp. 278, 280.
2. Jayaprakash Narayan, *Face to Face* (Sarva Seva Sangh Prakashan, Varanasi, 1970), p. 26.
3. *Maitri* (a Hindi monthly), May 1974, p. 322.
4. ibid.
5. *Harijan*, June 12, 1954, p. 122.
6. *Harijan*, November 29, 1953, p. 340.
7. Vinoba's attitude towards Satyagraha in the form of nonviolent resistance has been discussed by the author in his "Vinoba and Satyagraha", *Gandhi Marg*, October 1980.
8. *Sarvodaya*, July-August 1975 (additional pages).
9. *Bhoodan*, May 15, 1961. T.K. Oommen is of the same view, though he is highly critical of some aspects of the movement in his "Twenty-five Years of Bhoodan-Gramdan", in *Everyman's*, June 15, 1975.
10. *Bhoodan and the Landless* (Popular Prakashan, Bombay, 1973), p. 94.
11. *Sarvodaya*, April-June 1975, p. 447.
12. *Bhoodan Yajna*, Special Issue, April 18, 1963, pp. 108-09.
13. *Bhoodan*, December 23, 1957, p. 1.
14. A.W. Sahasrabuddhe, *Report on Koraput Gramdans* (Sevagram, n.d.), p. 19.
15. Vasant Vyas, *Tamilnad Mein Gramdan* (Sarva Seva Sangh Prakashan, Varanasi, 1965). Vyas has also reported on Gramdan in a few other States. But the only methodical study is of T. K. Oommen of Rajasthan Gramdans in *Charisma, Stability, and Change* (New Delhi, 1975). The results of his study are more or less negative, positive aspects having been underestimated. Detlef Kantowsky attributes it to a lack of a very sympathetic view of Sarvodaya

approach. See his *Sarvodaya: The Other Development* (Vikas Publishing House, New Delhi, 1980), p. 86.

16. This statement is based on the original U.P. legislation for the abolition of the Zamindari system, considered to be the best of all such legislations. Under it the landless agricultural labour had no claims on uncultivated lands vesting in the village.
17. T.K. Oommen, however, has found fault for making Bhoodan workers generate their own means of livelihood and for ambivalent attitude towards organization and discipline. See *Everyman's*, June 15, 1975. These changes have been made to increase the element of nonviolence in the movement to make it more effective.